Fuerteventura Island

Travel and Tourism, Family travel, Vacation, Honeymoon Holiday

Author
John Knight

Copyright Notice

Copyright © 2017 Global Print Digital
All Rights Reserved

Digital Management Copyright Notice. This Title is not in public domain, it is copyrighted to the original author, and being published by **Global Print Digital**. No other means of reproducing this title is accepted, and none of its content is editable, neither right to commercialize it is accepted, except with the consent of the author or authorized distributor. You must purchase this Title from a vendor who's right is given to sell it, other sources of purchase are not accepted, and accountable for an action against. We are happy that you understood, and being guided by these terms as you proceed. Thank you

First Printing: 2017.

ISBN: 978-1-912483-03-7

Publisher: Global Print Digital.
Arlington Row, Bibury, Cirencester GL7 5ND
Gloucester
United Kingdom.
Website: www.homeworkoffer.com

Table of Content

Introduction 1
History 3
Travel and Tourism 9
Activities and Locations 11
    Most Family-Friendly Activities in Fuerteventura 13
    Family Holiday 16
    Five fantastic ways Fuerteventura's an ideal hiking destination 19
    Fuerteventura Restaurants Leading Restaurants that you can use 23
    Fuerteventura, Your itinerary Days 28
    From Beach Resort to UNESCO Biosphere Reserve 33
    Isla Lobos, Fuerteventura 36
        Isla de Lobos, an idyllic day trip from Fuerteventura 39
    Driving on Fuerteventura, discovering northern highlights 42
    Driving on Fuerteventura, discovering the southern sights 44
    Five or more hot things to do on Fuerteventura 47
    Golf on Fuerteventura 52
        Work on that swing of yours on Fuerteventura's golf courses 55
    Morro Jable, Fuerteventura 59
    Cofete, Fuerteventura 61
    Puerto del Rosario, Fuerteventura 63
    Ajuy, Fuerteventura 67
    Corralejo Fuerteventura 68
    Costa Calma, Fuerteventura 71
    El Cotillo, Fuerteventura 74
    Costa Caleta, Fuerteventura 78
    Jandia, Fuerteventura 79
    Antigua, Fuerteventura 81
    Costa Antigua, Fuerteventura 83
    Caleta Paraiso, Costa Antigua, Fuerteventura. 86
    Giniginamar, Fuerteventura 87
    Gran Tarajal, Fuerteventura 88
    Lajares, Fuerteventura 89

- La Oliva, Fuerteventura 90
- Municipalities of Fuerteventura 91
- Tarajalejo, Fuerteventura 95
- Villaverde, Fuerteventura 96
- A walk up Pico de la Zarza, Morro Jable, Fuerteventura 97
- Tamaragua, Fuerteventura 98
- La Pared, Fuerteventura 99
- Las Playitas, Fuerteventura 100
- Tindaya Fuerteventura 101
- The Villa Winter 103
- Parque Holandes, Fuerteventura 107
- Tetir, Fuerteventura 109
- Triquivijate, Fuerteventura 110
- Puerto Lajas, Fuerteventura 111
- Betancuria, Fuerteventura 111
- Pozo Negro, Fuerteventura 114
- Ajuy, Fuerteventura 114

Beaches *115*
- La Concha beach on the Isle of Lobos 115
- Viejo Rey beach 116
- Corralejo's Big Beaches (Grandes Playas de Corralejo) 117
- La Guirra 118
- Cofete beach 119
- Esquinzo Butihondo beach 120
- La Guirra 121
- Morro Jable beach 122
- Sotavento beach 123
- La Concha beach, El Cotillo 124
- Corralejo Viejo 125
- Costa Calma beach 125

Weather in Fuerteventura *126*

Accommodation: Hotel and Beach Resort *128*
- Barceló Castillo Beach Resort 128
- ClubHotel Riu Oliva Beach Resort 129
- Iberostar Fuerteventura Palace 131

Hotel Riu Palace Tres Islas 133
Iberostar Playa Gaviotas 135
H10 Tindaya 137
Excursions on Fuerteventura and Lanzarote *139*
Fuerteventura Airport. *146*

Introduction

Fuerteventura is in the Canary Islands and measures 210 kilometres from one end to the other. It is outstanding for its magnificent white sand beaches and for the bright sun that shines all year round.

It is an essential destination for *windsurfing* and scuba diving lovers. Here you will find unforgettable spots. There are more than 150 beaches in the north and south of the island, spread over 340 kilometres of coastline. Meanwhile, on the east coast you will find cliffs and small, hidden coves.

Their shallow, crystal clear waters are ideal for watersports: sailing, water skiing, surfing, fishing... and, above all, *windsurfing*: the island now has an important place on the windsurfing World Cup circuit. There is a long list of beaches where you can practise this sport: Corralejo, Cotillo, Jandía, Caleta de Fuste, Cofete...

This is also the case for scuba diving. Fuerteventura is an ideal destination for diving fans, thanks to the crevices, caves, tunnels, overhangs and rock formations to be found on its ocean beds. Its excellent climate, sandy beaches with dunes, stunning natural beauty and modern infrastructure make Fuerteventura a privileged destination for tourists.

A good way to get to know the island's most hidden spots is to explore the tracks and trails that will lead you to areas of unspoilt countryside. This is the case of Tindaya Mountain and the Betancuria Nature Reserve, the island's largest area of protected countryside.

Fuerteventura airport is five kilometres from Puerto del Rosario, with services by airlines from many different countries. The island also has scheduled boat and ferry services to the rest of the archipelago, departing from Puerto del Rosario, La Oliva and Pájara.

History

Fuerteventura History

Fuerteventura, like the rest of the Canary islands, was inhabited by a primitive pagan people prior to its invasion by Europeans, although what to call this ancient people still remains a contentious issue.

Most Canarians call their ancestors 'Guanches' although strictly speaking this refers to a specific tribe from Tenerife. 'Mahorero' is still used today to describe the people of Fuerteventura and comes from the ancient word 'mahos' meaning a type of goatskin shoe worn by the original inhabitants.

Analysis of prehistoric remains (pictured) seem to indicate that this people arrived from North Africa, and this is borne out by many linguistic similarities between pre-hispanic place names, words and the language of the Berbers in North Africa.

Fuerteventura was known as Herbania, possibly a reference to it's abundant plant-life in ancient times (hard though it is to believe now looking at it's barren thirsty landscape) but more likely from the Berber word 'bani' meaning wall. A low wall spanned the narrowest width of the island, from La Pared (which means wall in Spanish) over to the east coast, dividing it into two kingdoms.

The North, Maxorata was ruled by Guize and Jandia in the South, by Ayoze. Although ostensibly ruled by these two kings, they in turn took advice and guidance from a mother and daughter team of two priestesses, Tibiabin and Tamonante.

It is thought that it was a polygamous society, with each woman having on average three husbands.

Their people lived on fish and shellfish, goats' meat, milk and cheese, and 'gofio' a finely ground toasted barley flour, all of which you will still find on the supermarket shelves today.

They lived in caves or semi-subterranean dwellings a few of which have been discovered and excavated, uncovering some examples of early tools and pottery. They were a spiritual people. The highest mountains provided the setting for pagan rituals and ceremonies. Engravings and religious symbols found on Mount Tindaya indicate this was one such sacred mountain

The Conquest of Fuerteventura

As was often the case, the salvation of pagan souls and the hope of discovering the source of Saharan gold, provided the motive for the conquest.

It was actually a Frenchman by the name of Jean de Bethencourt (right)who invaded Fuerteventura in 1402. After the initial complement of 280 French settlers was reduced by desertions to an eventual 63, Bethencourt transferred his allegiance to the king of Castille, where he had cousins by marriage, using Castille and especially Seville as recruiting grounds to meet his manpower needs.

Thus the island's Spanish heritage was created, with the French influence reduced to a few Castillianised versions of French place names such as Morro Jable (from the French 'sable' meaning sand), La Oliva (the olive tree) and Betancuria, the inland capital founded by Jean de Bethencourt. Indeed the island's name itself is said to be a Spanish adaptation of Bethencourt's exclamation 'Que forte aventure!

It was not until 1405 that Fuerteventura was finally conquered, largely due to the influence of the two priestesses, who persuaded Ayoze and Guize, the two kings, to surrender and accept baptism .They were each given some land and exemption from tribute payments for nine years. Whether the rest of the native population was assimilated or sold into slavery is a moot point, although the fact that many native words and techniques have survived to this day, suggests the former.

Now colonisation began in earnest, starting with the creation of the island's capital at Betancuria, situated in a fertile inland valley, and less prone to pirate attacks than it's vulnerable coastline. Here, the masons brought with him from France, built the island's first church, the Santa Maria de Betancuria where the islanders' spiritual needs were catered for. A tithe of 10% of all merchandise and agricultural produce was payable to the church and 20% to the ruler of the island.

Jean de Bethencourt returned to Normandy, leaving the island under the administration of his nephew. By virtue of sale or inheritance the island passed from ruler to ruler, eventually being inherited by the Herrera-Perazas and remaining under the feudal rule of this family for the next three centuries. Despite the subjugation of the natives, these were by no means peaceful times.

Portugal had a covetous eye on both Lanzarote and Fuerteventura, mounting an expedition in 1460 to invade them. Coastal villages remained vulnerable to pirate attacks, forcing their inhabitants to seek refuge in the mountains. Furthermore, a tempting supply of a precious commodity slaves- lay a mere 80kms across the sea. Frequent raids were mounted providing a steady supply of slaves, camels and livestock, both for sale and domestic use. However this in turn, invited retaliatory attacks by the Moors.

In 1593 one such attack razed the island. The church at Betancuria was burnt down, villages were plundered, captives taken and hefty ransoms demanded to release them from the dungeons of Fez.

After many decades of resistance, the natives on the fertile island of Gran Canaria were eventually conquered in 1483, coming under the direct rule of the crown. Fuerteventura, with its intermediate lordships and subsequent higher taxes, in addition to its dry, barren landscape was therefore a much less attractive propositon to potential settlers. It found itself largely bypassed by the economic booms experienced in Gran Canaria and Tenerife, who became the gateway for trade between the Americas and Europe.

Gradually life seems to have become a little more stable, with the creation in the 1700s of six new parishes. In 1708 the Regiment of militias was created, headed by the colonels. They took up residence in La Oliva, which became the military and civil capital of the island.

The colonels wielded considerable power, choosing the mayor and exiling anyone who dared to oppose them. For more than a century, marriages were arranged between the colonels' family members, effectively forming a closed circle. The Casa de Los Coroneles still stands as testament to this village's past military splendour. The town of Antigua briefly became capital of the island in 1808, but more importantly became the focus for opposition to the feudal system, fomenting dissent amongst the people in the South.

A period of conflict followed, between supporters of the colonels and the feudal system in the North, and those opposed to it in the South. Eventually in 1835 the feudal system was abolished and each parish was made into an administrative district. In 1820 the port at Puerto de Cabras (now Puerto del Rosario) had been declared the principal port of the island and in 1835 it took over the mantle of capital of the island.

Travel and Tourism

Whether you're thinking of taking your holidays in Fuerteventura, booking a hotel, hiring a car, booking a Cheap Flight to Fuerteventura looking for more information or simply reading for fun, let us simply welcome you to this beautiful Canary island. Be assured that you will have every information you need for Fuerteventura travel and tourism in this book

With three thousand hours of sunshine a year, Fuerteventura is the closest Canary Island to the African coast with only 100km separating the 'Punta de la Entallada' from Cape Juby in Morroco and is the second largest (after Tenerife) of all the islands.

The weather conditions of Fuerteventura are very similar to Florida and Mexico which are on the same latitude, which make this island the ideal holiday location.

There is no other island in the Canaries with as many enormous sand dunes and long sandy beaches (more than one hundred and fifty). Even though most of the land on Fuerteventura consists of stone and rock, this island has some of the most impressive beaches in the whole of Europe. Approx 98km long and 30km across at the widest point.

In the history of time Fuerteventura is generally regarded as the oldest of all the Canaries and its strange contours come from various volcanic episodes. The last eruption occurred about 7,000 years ago so you're pretty safe! Should you wish to see some volcanic activity take a trip to the neighboring island of Lanzarote, it's well worth the effort. See our Ferry page for details on how to get there. You can also take a short boat trip over to the small island of Los Lobos (only 6sqkm) and really get away from it all.

Water sports are very popular in Fuerteventura. Every year hundreds of surfers, windsurfers, kitesurfers, and divers descend on Fuerteventura and during July the island is host to the P.W.A world windsurfing speed and slalom event at Sotavento in the south.

There are many new attractions inviting tourists to discover different aspects of the Island's landscape and culture such as the Betancuria Museum of Archaeology and Ethnography and Tefia Craft Village to name but a few.

Read through this book and see what's on offer. Its miles and miles of broad sandy beaches and golden sand dunes make Fuerteventura the ideal holiday resort for everyone.

Activities and Locations

The island of Fuerteventura

Fuerteventura is more relaxed than some of the other Canary Islands, and this makes it an ideal place for those of us that prefer a quieter life. It is only recently that the people on Fuerteventura has outnumbered the goats.

The large number of white sandy beaches around the coastline of sunny Fuerteventura act as a magnet for people from all over Europe. The sea conditions vary from beach to beach. Some are more suitable for surfers, whilst others provide safe bathing for all the family. Sea life is abundant around the coasts of Fuerteventura and it is always worth packing a mask and snorkel, if you like to look at the fish and other aquatic organisms, or a rod if you would prefer to go fishing.

The planners on Fuerteventura have been able to look at the way the other Canary Islands developed. They seem keen to maintain a balance between the development needed to cater for the increasing popularity of the island, and a desire to preserve the island's quintessential charm and character. There was a lot of building of villas , hotels and holiday complexes in the first half of the last decade, but since then the development has slowed right down. Most development is no higher than two storeys and has been concentrated in existing towns and villages, leaving rural Fuerteventura very much the same as it was.

Fuerteventura airport is located on the east coast of the island. The nearest holiday resort is Caleta de Fuste, which is about 6km to south. A convenient distance for those of us that live there.

Besides activities you would expect at the seaside in a sunny place, there are plenty of others ways of spending time on the island. These include a number of museums, a zoo and botanical gardens, three 1 8 hole golf courses and one hole course , and of course the island itself.

Fuerteventura's Weather and its name.
You might have heard that Fuerteventura means strong wind, and it is true that the island is in the path of the trade winds, which makes for great watersports. It is just as likely to have derived from the French for Strong Adventure! Anyway, Fuerteventura is one of the

sunniest places on earth, the sun shines here for around 3000 hours a year!

Most Family-Friendly Activities in Fuerteventura
1. Go to the Zoo

One of the more popular family-friendly activities in Fuerteventura is Oasis Park, in Caleta de Fuste. The zoo is home to over 3,000 animals and you can see 250 different species. You can get up close and personal with many of the animals, and a highlight is being able to feed a number of the zoo's inhabitants, including giraffes, elephants and zebras.

There are various shows you can see, such as a Reptiles Show, Sea Lion Show and Birds of Prey Show. And younger children will love the small farm, where they can see animals such as goats, emus, ostriches, turtles and ducks. There is also a children's playground for when you need a break from seeing the animals.

It is also home to the Fuerteventura Botanical Garden, one of the largest cactus botanical gardens in Europe.

Open all year from 9am to 6pm. Cost is 33 Euros for adults and 19.50 Euros for children (ages 5-11). Children under 5 are free. The zoo offers a free bus service for visitors from around the island, meaning you don't need a car to get there.

2. Watersports

With its fantastic sandy beaches and island winds, Fuerteventura is the ideal place for your family to try its hand at some watersports. Surfing is popular in the north of the island and windsurfing in the south, with Jandia playing host to the World Windsurfing Championships in July.

The clear waters make it an ideal spot for some snorkelling or scuba diving and you can easily hire the equipment you need locally. For fishing enthusiasts, try out some deep-sea fishing on a marlin sea-fishing trip.

Many hotels have on-site watersports facilities and there are several independent schools located around the island. For a list of children's schools

3. Go on Safari

Camel safaris, Jeep safaris, dolphin safaris and submarines safaris Fuerteventura offers you a wide choice of ways to go on safari!

Camel and Jeep safaris are a great way to explore the island and many tour operators and hotels can arrange one of these trips for you.

If you would prefer to be out to sea, you can take a boat trip and, if you're lucky, see some dolphins and whales. Or for something a bit different, go on a **submarine safari**, a unique experience that combines both surface and submerged travelling. It departs from Morro Jable, in the south of the island, and you could see a whole range aquatic creatures, including sea turtles, barracudas and sting rays, all in their natural environment.

4. Visit a Nature Park

Corralejo Nature Park is located just outside Corralejo in the north of Fuerteventura and is said to be like stepping into the Sahara (which is actually only about 60 miles away). It's made up of 24 acres of sand dunes along a 7km stretch of beach and is an ever-changing landscape thanks to the winds that shape the dunes.

It's free day out (although you may want to hire one of the sun loungers and umbrellas available) and the children will have great fun running through the dunes. They may even spot one of the local geckos or lizards. Although the wind, sand and sun cream combination may get a bit annoying for parents!

5. Take a Boat Trip to Los Lobos Island

Los Lobos Island, named after the seals (sea wolves) that used to inhabit the island, is located off the coast of Corralejo. There are daily boat trips to the island, where you can spend the day relaxing on the beach or paddling in the clear waters.

Family Holiday

With the promise of warm weather all year without having to do a long-haul flight, Fuerteventura is a popular destination for a family holiday. So here is our quick guide to going on a family holiday in Fuerteventura, the second largest island of the Canary Islands.

When to go

Summers in Fuerteventura are warm and dry, with average temperatures of around 25°C. However, the mercury can comfortably hit the 30s in July and August, which may be a little too warm for some children. As the weather remains relatively warm the rest of the year though, it's great if you are looking for a family holiday outside of peak season. There is more rainfall outside of the summer months, with March, October and December being the wettest months but still nowhere near as wet as the UK!

Where to stay

We went to Fuerteventura when Sophie was just 10 months old and stayed on the North of the island, in Corralejo. We spent a week in a one-bedroom apartment at the Oasis Papagayo and had a great time.

Corralejo itself is a popular resort but still manages to retain some of its traditional fishing village charm. Costa Caleta is close to the airport and is a good option for watersports and golf enthusiasts. To the South of the island there is Jandia, which enjoys a beautiful white sandy beach, which is also a popular choice for watersports and mixes modern hotels and bars with the more traditional side of Fuerteventura. See our recommended Fuerteventura hotels for some family-friendly hotel suggestions.

Family Time

With over 125 miles of sandy beaches, including six Blue Flag beaches, Fuerteventura is perfect for families who love spending time on the beach. And, with its strong winds, it is also a great location for watersports and kite-surfing for the more adventurous family members. But for those families looking to spend some time away from the beach, there is still plenty on offer. For animal lovers, there is Oasis Park, a zoo and botanical gardens home to over 3,000 animals and 250 species. Or discover a taste of the Sahara with a visit to the expansive sand dunes of Parque Natural de las Dunas, in Corralejo. And, if you happen to be in the region of Cofete beach in August, why not join in the releasing back into the sea of sea turtles that have hatched on the beach.

You Time

Although Fuerteventura is a great destination for a family holiday, it also offers parents the chance to enjoy some "me-time" if you're able to take advantage of a kids' club or tag team the childcare for a few hours. For golf lovers, there are some fantastic golf courses, with Fuerteventura Golf Club being one of the most popular, having hosted the Spanish Open in 2004. For those looking for a more relaxing treat, there are some wonderful spas on the island, often linked to a hotel. So if your own hotel doesn't have one or if you are staying in a villa, a nearby hotel is sure to offer you the chance to escape for a few hours.

Local Treats

The food in Fuerteventura is very Spanish-influenced and features a lot of seafood. A popular fish is the local Parrot Fish (*Vieja*), which is often served salted. They are also very fond of goat and goat's cheese, from which the local speciality cheese, Majorero Cheese (*Queso Majorero*), is made. And of course there is the Fuerteventuran version of the Canarian favourite, *mojo picón* sauce. This slightly spicy sauce is usually made from olive oil, vinegar, paprika and garlic but there are many variations of the recipe.

Good to Know

- ✓ Fuerteventura's official language is Spanish but English (and German) is widely spoken in tourist areas.
- ✓ Menu prices usually include service but most people leave a tip and 5% is considered reasonable.
- ✓ It can be windy on the island (the name "Fuerteventura" roughly translates as "strong winds") so be careful in the sun as it may feel cooler than it actually is.
- ✓ The emergency number is 112.
- ✓ The time zone is GMT+1.
- ✓ Although there is a good bus service in Fuerteventura, car hire is recommended for those wanting to explore the island beyond the more popular towns.

Five fantastic ways Fuerteventura's an ideal hiking destination

For sure, Fuerteventura's 150 and more beaches are a big draw and probably the reason you booked a holiday on the island in the first place. However, there's so much more to see and do on Fuerteventura. And a great way of discovering what else the island has to offer is to take a ride on Shanks' pony.

Your (hiking) boots were made for walking, after all. So save some space for them when it comes to packing your suitcase. Here are five reasons why Fuerteventura's such a perfect place to trek. Now which one(s) will tempt you to part with your sunlounger?

1. There are more goats than people

Once upon a time, Fuerteventura's current capital wasn't called Puerto del Rosario (Rosary Port) but Puerto de Cabras (Goat Port). The locals, sick of being a laughing stock, brought pressure on the local government to force through a name change in 1956. Although the goat's still very much a revered symbol of the island, with the locals milking the 20+ varieties to produce what's been described as "the best goats' cheese in the world."

With around only 90,000 people living on the second largest of the Canary Islands, it's easy to get away from it all. Head into the interior to evade the bucket-and-spade brigade. Although just when you're lulled into thinking you could quite possibly be the last remaining survivor on Planet Earth, the tinkling of the bells on grazing goats will rouse you from your reverie.

2.) Start or end your hikes in beautiful hamlets

Considering Fuerteventura's capital houses just over 35,000 inhabitants, the island's decidedly more rural than urban. A case in point is picturesque Vega de Río Palmas in the centre of the island, whose church is photographed above. Located in the *Barranco de la Vega*, the abundant palm trees offer some much-needed shelter.

More experienced hikers will rise to the challenge of the near-16km trek to the fishing village of Ajuy on Fuerteventura's west coast. On the way, you'll pass the island's most well-known chapel, Nuestra Señora de la Peña. As well as the Presa de las Peñitas, a clogged dam just over 3.5km into your walk.

3.) The views

Talking of Presa de las Peñitas, here's some photographic evidence of the eye candy this part of Fuerteventura has in store for you. That's what 265 metres of elevation gives you. Great vistas and a souvenir for you to capture on your camera.

If it's a hike with a view you're after, take the trek which connects the two municipal capitals of Antigua and Betancuria. Totalling just over 3km, you'll be able to see mountainous trio, Bermeja, La Ventosilla, and Tindaya. A short detour will take you to the Mirador de Morro Veloso, perched on top of the 669m-tall Montaña Tegú.

4.) It's safe

Crime exists everywhere on the planet but away from the resorts where pickpockets have been known to operate, inland Fuerteventura poses little threat. It's a far cry from Madeira where thieves have homed in on the easy target of hikers trekking the narrow paths along the *levadas* (canals). To ensure the safest of hikes, travel light but with the essentials of sensible shoes, sun protection, and water.

What also makes Fuerteventura safe as a hiking destination. Its all-year-round spring-like temperatures means that there's not really a off season on the trekking front as there is, say, in Andalucia. Although, it's probably best to attempt shorter rather than longer hikes in the height of summer.

5.) You can go up in the world without suffering vertigo
The highest point on Fuerteventura's Pico de la Zarza. Located on the Jandía peninsula, this peak reaches a height of 807 metres. So, it will suit amateur hikers as it's not challenging as trekking on the likes of La Gomera and La Palma. And who doesn't want to play "I'm the king of the castle" on Montaña Tindaya above? Just 401 metres to climb, guys.

And you can reach other high points along Fuerteventura's 255km of hiking paths. So where will you go. Along the coast, into the lunar lanscape, through the desert? The choice is yours

Fuerteventura Restaurants Leading Restaurants that you can use

Comfort eating's an option in Fuerteventura. Tucking into grub you like to enjoy at home. Yet whilst you're away, how about letting your taste buds play with some new flavour sensations? However, our top 10 restaurants in Fuerteventura offer some familiar cuisine alongside the more unfamiliar. In no particular order, they are as follows.

Cantante Cafe

Take a head chef who's worked under the Michelin-starred Mark Hix in the UK, mix in locally-sourced produce, and you end up with Cantante Cafe's innovative gourmet menu. Short on quantity of dishes, it's long on quality. Enjoy a meal with a view, as you can survey the neighbouring islands of Lanzarote and Lobos from the vantage point of your table.

Contact details: Paseo Atlantico 2, 35660, Corralejo. 928 537 357.

Opening hours: *Monday to Sunday*: 9:00am - 2:00am

2.) Restaurante Marabu

Unlucky for you if your holiday on Fuerteventura's during the first week of December, the last week of January, or from the third week of June through to the end of the July. For these periods mark Restaurante Marabu's *vacaciones*. If your vacation doesn't coincide with the restaurants's, you'll be able to yummy down on sumptuously-prepared Mediterranean cuisine in an ambient setting.

Contact details: Calle Fuente de Hija, 35626, Morro Jable/Esquinzo. 928 544 098.

Opening hours: *Monday to Saturday*: 1:00pm - 11:00pm

3.) La Arroceria
La Arroceria reminds you that whilst the African coast lies just 100km away, Fuerteventura's very much Spain. So, you'll be able to feast on the finest Valencian paellas and rice dishes from Alicante. Washed down with a glass or two of Bocopa's fine wine.

Contact details: Calle Pejin 10, 35660, Corralejo. 928 535 291.

Opening hours: *Monday to Sunday*: 12:30pm - 10:30pm

4.) Casa Toño
Although red tuna's a speciality, the food prepared by rising star of Spanish cooking, Toño Alonso, is as about the turf as much as the surf. And so goat and ox turn up on the menu. And for lovers of an after-dinner drink, the only dilemma will be which of the more than 40 gins to choose to accompany your tonic.

Contact details: Calle Alcalde Alonso Patallo 8, 35600, Puerto del Rosario. 928 344 736.

Opening hours: *Monday to Saturday*: 12:00pm - 12:00am

5.) Land of Freedom

Land of Freedom? Is it a pub, restaurant, or wine bar? In truth, it's probably all three rolled into one. A new addition to the Fuerteventura gastronomic scene, this eatery only opened in summer 2014. And wherever you come from, you should be able to understand the menu; seeing as it's been painstakingly translated into 48 different languages.

Ostensibly specializing in Italian cuisine, Land of Freedom are committed to the slow-food philosophy. They offer tasting trays with five dishes paired with five wines (or juices for kids). Themes include land, sea, and vegetarian. If you then want a larger portion of something you've sampled, the kitchen are happy to prepare it for you. Although as yet there have been no takers; with visitors reserving space for dessert.

Contact details: Urbanización Lobos Bahia Local 5, Avenida Nuestra Señora del Carmen, 35660, Corralejo. 928 867 732.

Opening hours: *Monday to Saturday*: 9:30am - 11:30pm

6.) Restaurante Mahoh

Housed in an early 19th-century rural abode, Restaurante Mahoh takes its name from an old aboriginal word meaning "My land, my country." Mahoh's also the appelation for an environmental group set up to preserve Fuerteventura's landscape. Its president's restaurant owner, Tinín Martinez.

It's a family affair at Restaurante Mahoh with Martinez' son in law Victor Curbelo acting as the maître d'hôtel. A temple to classic Canarian fare, the menu features such staples as *potaje de berros*(watecress stew), *papas arrugadas con mojo picón* (salty boiled new potatoes with spicy sauce) and *baifo* (goat). The restaurant's beautiful garden displays flora both endemic and imported to the island.

Contact details: Calle Francisco Bordón Méndez 1, Sitio Juan Bello, 35640, Villaverde. 928 868 050.

Opening hours: *Monday to Tuesday and Thursday to Sunday (closed Wednesdays)* 1.00pm - 12:00am

7.) Rojo Tomate

There are more than red tomatoes to eat at this family-run pizzeria. And not only green peppers. Chef Alberta lovingly prepares everything on the menu, from the *focaccias* available as starters through to the fresh pasta and later the meringues which accompany your post-meal coffee.

Contact details: Calle La Cancela 8, 35650, Lajares. 928 861 513.

Opening hours: *Tuesday to Sunday*: 6:00pm - 11:00pm

8.) The Ugly Duckling
Small but perfectly formed Scandinavian restaurant marries style with substance. See what all the fuss is about regarding Danish cuisine without paying the sky-high prices of the likes of Copenhagen's Noma. A recently-updated wine list features vintages from Lanzarote's leading wineries.

Contact details: Calle Isla de Lobos 2, 35660, Corralejo. 618 044 896.

Opening hours: Open for dinner only. Times vary from week to week. Call to reserve in advance.

9.) La Vaca Azul
Settings don't get much more special than La Vaca Azul's on the old harbourfront in El Cotillo. This seafood restaurant does a mean paella, as you can see in the picture above. Vegetarians, though, will prefer the local majorero cheese which is battered and then fried before being served with a dipping jam.

Contact details: Calle Requena 9, 35650, El Cotillo. 928 538 685.

Opening hours: *Monday to Sunday*: 10:00am - 10:00pm

10.) Baobab Juice Bar Casa Vegetariana
Veggies will be even more spoiled for choice at Baobab Juice Bar Casa Vegetariana which is so (pure) vegetarian-friendly, it's actually vegan. Unlucky not to make the cut for our top 10 vegetarian restaurants in Spain, it goes big on the usual suspects to be found in an organic

larder. So, expect to see plenty of cous cous, seitan, tofu, and tempeh on the menu.

Most of the decor's at this relaxed restaurant's recycled. There's an emphasis on fat-free breakfasts, lunches, and snacks. So make your way to Baobab Juice Bar Casa Vegetariana if you want to get fit rather than fat on a Fuerteventura holiday.

Contact details: Calle José Seguro Torres 14, 35660, Corralejo.

Opening hours: *Monday to Saturday*: 10:00am - 5:00pm

Fuerteventura, Your itinerary Days

Fuerteventura's a short-haul paradise island, boasting many of Europe's best beaches. You could easily spend a week here, lazing in the all-year-round sun. Or you could go explore, ticking items off our Fuerteventura bucket list as you do.

Day one: Hit the north on Fuerteventura

There can be little argument that Corralejo tops Fuerteventura's top 10 beaches. And debate might be just as scant regarding its position in a list of the finest beaches across all Canary Islands. And given the quality of Canarian playas, that's some achievement.

Corralejo's beach stretches to 10km. Meaning there's plenty of room for families, surfers and, indeed, nudists. Located in the north-east of the island, Corralejo's also home to one of Fuerteventura's major resorts. And using the FV-1, it's a near 40-km, 40-minute drive from the island's airport.

Day two: Unlock the promise of the east

Day two, how about spending some more time on a beach? Well, that's what Fuerteventura's famous for, after all, and you're on holiday. Pictured above is Caleta de Fuste aka El Castillo, a near 45-minute drive along the FV-1 from Corralejo.

Caleta de Fuste's your classic horseshoe-shaped beach. Although there's nothing traditional about its texture, with the sand imported rather than homegrown. Active types will enjoy the diving, sailing and windsurfing opportunities, whilst the more leisurely traveller might want to go out on a boat, or even submarine, trip.

If you want a break from the resorts, head to Gran Tarajal. This is a town where locals live, some of which you'll see fishing for a living on a walk along the parade. And, yes, there's also a 800-metre-long beach to visit if you fancy a spot of sunbathing.

Day three: Get out of your comfort zone in the south

North, south, east, west; you're never far from a beach on Fuerteventura. The island's stunning coastline's home to more than 150 beaches. One of the most acclaimed's Sotavento. It's not difficult to see why, even if only based on the evidence of the photo above. Perhaps the setting will inspire you to try a new challenge; maybe giving windsurfing a go for the first time?

But for a break from the beach, how about visiting Fuerteventura's highest point? 807 metres tall, the Pico de Zarza's a four-hour up-and-down hike. A wide track gives easy access, but as you reach the summit be careful of the conditions which can get quite windy at times. Look west for the village of Cofete and its 14-km beach whilst glancing east, you'll be able to make out holy mountain, Montaña del Cardón.

Day four: Enjoy a day out in the wild west

The coast around the isolated fishing village of Ajuy, as you can clearly see depicted in the photo above, is more rough than smooth. It's this rocky western shoreline which French explorer Jean de Béthencourt moored his fleet at in 1402. With his band of 280 settlers reduced by desertion to 63, Béthencourt contacted the Spanish royal family to recruit extra manpower. The island would fall to this Norman conqueror three years later.

At Fuerteventura's west coast, you'll see the Atlantic Ocean at its roughest and readiest. It's here where US ocean liner SS America ran aground in January 1994. Over 20 years later, due to the gradual disintegration of the ship, you can now only see what's left of the wreck at low tide.

For a very different experience than that offered by the resorts, travel to Los Molinos. You won't have any choice on the restaurant front, hola Casa Pon, but you'll mingle with locals rather than tourists as you tuck into Canarian rather than international fayre. Casa Pon's open seven days a week, from Monday to Friday, 10:00am to 6:00pm, and Saturdays and Sunday 10:00am to 7:00pm (10:00pm) in summer months.

Day five: Visit Fuerteventura's centre point

Antigua's one of Fuerteventura's oldest villages. Dating back to the 18th century, it was capital of the island for all of a year. Antigua's windmill has been restored to its former glory and now's home to a cultural centre which has proved a popular tourist attraction.

There's not that much to see and do in Antigua, but what there is remains special. The main square's a botantic garden in miniature, with resplendent flora blooming all year round. Look out for the church, the Iglesia de Nuestra Señora which started life as a basic hermitage.

Day six: Explore Puerto del Rosario

Will a population of under 40,000, Puerto del Rosario's more capital town than capital city. Nevertheless, all roads lead there on Fuerteventura. As it's so well connected, with a regular bus service from and to various locations, it makes for an ideal day trip.

Puerto del Rosario's been capital of Fuerteventura since 1860. Up until 1956, however, its name was Puerto de Cabras (Port of Goats). To this day, there are more goats on the island than people with the locals putting the goat's milk lake to good use by producing the Manchegoesque Majorero, a cheese that's popular with purists.

Very much a working town, nevertheless Puerto del Rosario has been beautified in recent years. More than 100 sculptures dating back to the late 1990s and early 21st century line the streets. A more historic tourist attraction is the Casa-Museo Unamuno which chronicles the time celebrated Spanish intellectual Miguel Unamuno spent on the island after being exiled there by dictator Primo de Rivera in 1924.

Day seven: Head to Betancuria
Our old friend Jean de Béthencourt had a plan. He thought a capital would be safe from pirate attack if it was built inland. So, he founded a settlement and named it after his good self after finally winning control of Fuerteventura in 1405.

But this westerly village was more or less destroyed by Jaban, a pirate who it seems was as much landlubber as nautical whizz. Not that Béthencourt lived to see his namesake being razed to the ground, with the attack coming in 1593. Despite this, a rebuilt Betancuria remained capital until 1834.

From Beach Resort to UNESCO Biosphere Reserve

Think Fuerteventura and the first thing that pops into your mind will probably be the sort of endless golden beaches you daydream about. It is without a doubt the Canary Island with the best beaches of all. If you've actually visited Fuerteventura you might also conjure up goats, lots of them, wandering across arid plains.

Recently a tour guide who has worked and lived on a few of the Canary Islands remarked to me 'there's not much to see or do on Fuerteventura'.

I disagree. Fuerteventura is one of the most surprising of the Canary Islands. For years I dismissed it as more or less one big beach. I was wrong. It's a fascinating and beautiful island... and UNESCO agree.

Since 2009, the island has been a UNESCO Biosphere Reserve. In 2015 it was also recognised as a Starlight Reserve thanks to its dark skies filled with sparkling jewels rather than artificial light.

What is a UNESCO Biosphere Reserve?

To be designated a Biosphere Reserve, specific areas have to show that there is a strong historic link between man and nature. For a fuller explanation

Why is Fuerteventura a UNESCO Biosphere Reserve?

The oldest Canary Island has been shaped by nature for over 20 million years. Once it had mountains reaching as high as 3000m into the sky. Now its landscape is mainly made up of wide plains and softly curved hills, the highest of which is just over 800m. As a contrast, many of the walking routes I follow on Tenerife don't start until the 1000m above sea level mark.

The one big beach tag isn't that much of an exaggeration, according to UNESCO Fuerteventura has the largest desert in Europe. I walked some of it once, a sandy landscape that seemed to go on forever. It's not a habitat that makes life easy for farmers.

And yet within its hidden ravines are surprises; splashes of greenery and streams. There are olive trees, pistachios and palms. The western coast of Fuerteventura stretches for over 100 kilometres with hardly any human presence. It's a land with a surprising variety of bird-life, ranging from Cory's shearwaters to Bulwer's petrels and from kestrels to Egyptian vultures. Fossils show an even wider range of creatures now lost to the world, like the odd sounding lava mouse. On sacred mountains there are ancient engravings, whilst the orange landscape is peppered with lovely old windmills. It lies closest to Africa of all the Canary Islands and that gives it a different vibe.

Fuerteventura looks as though it has more in common with the continent lying to the east than its neighbouring islands to the west... and its night skies are black.

Fuerteventura Biosphere Reserve highlights

Although all of Fuerteventura is a UNESCO Biosphere Reserve, there are some sights which shouldn't be missed.

Isla de Lobos
Fuerteventura in miniature, the little Isla de Lobos near Corralejo is worth a day trip. Read the complete information on Isla de Lobos page

Betancuria
The former capital of the island and the prettiest town by far, Betancuria is packed with visitors during the day and like a dead zone after dark. Best way to explore its historic charms is under your own steam. Fit it into a driving tour of Fuerteventura's southern attractions.

A land of windmills

Although there are windmills dotted all over the island, the area between Antigua and Tiscamanita is good windmill hunting territory.

Those amber hills

There are excellent viewpoints across Fuerteventura, some of the best being on the road between Valle de Santa Ines and La Pared.

The beaches

You're not going to visit Fuerteventura and not spend time on a beach. This is Nirvana for beach bums. Whatever you heard about the Corralejo Dunes, or whatever images you've seen, nothing comes close to the reality of seeing them through your own eyes.

There might be more to Fuerteventura than its beaches, but the beaches *are* something special.

Isla Lobos, Fuerteventura

The island of Lobos is a nature reserve a ten minute ferry trip away from Corralejo, and just a little bit further from Lanzarote.

There is a visitors centre with information about the island, as well as a circular hall where people can go to get out of the sun and eat their picnics and escape from the sun.

There is also an archaeological site that is investigating the remains of a roman settlement that was on the island for the purpose of obtaining dye from mussels. Between spells of activity this is covered to stop the effects of weathering and to prevent sand accumulating over the digging that has already been done.

The island is small enough to be walked round in a few hours, but large enough for you to be able to feel that you are the only person on the island. The entire coastline is just under 14km.

The fact that the island is a nature reserve means that you are not free to tramp all over the island, but a series of well defined paths allows all of the island to be seen. There are rangers who will make sure you stick to the paths! The views from the top of The Caldera de la Montana are particularly rewarding, though they are not entirely free, as the 127m climb to the summit is too strenuous for some people.

On the day that we went there were wall to wall blue skies. The trip across on the ferry started at 9.45 and we were on the island at just after ten. Having made a short stop to observe the fish through the glass bottom of the boat.

We decide to tour the island in an anticlockwise direction, calling in at El Puertito to visit the restaurant. Unfortunately this was closed when we visited, so we carried on along the track, past the Playa de la Arena to the lighthouse. If you want to use the restaurant you have to book in advance.

There is a wide range of flora on the island. It got its name Lobos from the large population of seals "wolves of the sea" as they were called, that used to live there,

There is very little shade on the island, so it was pleasant to sit in the shade of the lighthouse, looking towards Lanzarote. There is something very relaxing about watching the Atlantic waves roll into the shores of Lobos.

Having rested a while we walked on towards the Caldera de la Montana. The climb here is quite steep and long enough to cause some visitors to turn back. This may have been because the path is made from hard rock that is fairly unforgiving if you are not wearing suitable footwear.

The views from the top are well worth the effort. There are excellent views of the island itself and you have a birds eye view of the surfers waiting for a suitable wave to roll in from the Atlantic.

When we got down from the mountain we walked to the beach at Playa de la Concha. This beach forms an arc around a cove, the water of which is shallow enough to be safe, and deep enough to enjoy.

We really enjoyed our trip to Lobos and would recommend it as an excellent day out. We would advise taking enough water and food to get through the day, and would also advise making sure you have adequate protection against the sun. If you tackle the mountain early on, then you can loll about for the rest of the day knowing you have earned your relaxation. Don't forget to take some sturdy footwear

Isla de Lobos, an idyllic day trip from Fuerteventura

A mere fifteen minutes boat trip from the Canary Island of Fuerteventura's most popular tourist resort, Corralejo, lies a tiny island populated for much of the year by a handful of grizzled old fishermen.

The Isla de Lobos is so small that it makes the Canary Island's other 'secret' island, La Graciosa near Lanzarote, seem like a bustling tourist hot spot.

Why visit Isla de Lobos?

I have to admit when I first heard about Isla de Lobos, I envisioned a golden sand paradise; a place to play your desert island discs and return to nature (i.e. expose all the white bits) a bit like La Graciosa in fact.

I expected the small ferry that transports visitors from the port at Corralejo to be jam packed with sunseekers looking for the perfect island beach a tall order given that Corralejo itself is famous for its dunas; miles and miles of undulating sand dunes, the sight of which automatically prompts the theme tune from Lawrence of Arabia to swirl in a mirage-like haze around your head (if you're of a certain age).

It wasn't. In fact, the small ferry wasn't even full.

Possibly what saves the Isla de Lobos from an influx of beach bums (as Fuerteventura is known for its naturist scene, take that phrase literally) is the fact that there aren't many beaches. And what there is can't match the endless stretch of gold on the other side of the narrow channel of water.

Isla de Lobos is better suited to hikers and those who want a fascinating insight into the simple life that existed (still exists in some places on the islands) before mass tourism changed the economic game plan. Fuerteventura itself is an untapped seam for walkers with a lot to offer those who like to explore places using leg power.

The ferry drops its passengers at a tiny jetty in what passes for the island's only settlement, El Puertito. By settlement I mean a handful of simple cottages dotted around beautiful sea pools. Some cottages are whitewashed with Greek blue doors and window frames, with others the dark volcanic boulders are left exposed and the cottages melt into the rough landscape. Some people live a simple life at El Puertito year round, but the hamlet bursts into life in the summer months when Fuerteventura 'mainlanders' decamp here.

There's also a good visitor centre, which helps put the diminutive island's existence into context and explain the name Isla de Lobos; the island of wolves. In this case it's sea wolves; a reference to the colony of monk seals that lived happily on the island until the post conquest settlers killed them all.

There are a number of interlinking paths which dissect and circumnavigate the island, all leading to little 'surprises' more inland pools; salt marshes; a lonely lighthouse with peeling plaster that makes it look as though it's been the victim of a shelling; salt pans whose empty basins expose only dry, cracked mud; a volcanic cone viewpoint that towers above the island and, finally, an idyllic little cove with soft sand and sparkling turquoise water.

Isla de Lobos is a beautiful little island; a surprising island and one of the highlights of any visit to Fuerteventura. It's just such a shame that there are no longer any seals basking in the hot sunshine.

The ferry to Isla de Lobos runs at regular times throughout the day (frequency depends on seasons) and costs around €15 return. For ideas about more day trips on Fuerteventura take a look at our discovering northern highlights and southern sights driving routes pages in this book

Driving on Fuerteventura, discovering northern highlights

The idea of sunbathing on a golden Fuerteventura beach seems a dream winter holiday activity when much of Northern Europe is trying to stay warm by turning the heating to high and wrapping up in woolly warmers. But here's another activity on Fuerteventura which is a joy, especially to someone like me who used to have to endure crawling along the motorway between Stockport and Salford Quays every morning driving.

The roads on Fuerteventura are relatively empty, in decent condition, not particularly winding (certainly not compared to the western Canary Islands) and are great for exploring on four wheels. For a relatively big island, it's the second largest of the Canary Islands, you can get from A to B surprisingly quickly and easily.

However, when you're taking a mini road trip it's better to take it slow and enjoy the scenery.

This is our suggestion for a driving route around the north of Fuerteventura.

From Corralejo to La Oliva

Take the FV101 out of Corralejo towards La Oliva/El Cotillo. It's a straightforward route all the way to La Oliva which has been an agricultural centre since around 1500. There's car parking beside the Church of Nuestra Señora de la Candelaria in the centre of the town. If it's a Tuesday there's a craft market in the town between 10am and 2pm otherwise there are a couple of places worth checking out. Casa de los Coroneles is located in a beautiful colonial mansion and features temporary and permanent exhibitions (entrance €4). Alternatively there's the Centro de Arte Canario which has cactus gardens, sculptures (some are a bit cheesy but fun) and works by famous Spanish artists (also €4).

La Oliva to El Cotillo

Follow the FV10 from La Oliva to El Cotillo which, although now a popular spot for surfers, also has a past. El Cotillo was once a centre for the production of orchilla, a plant used for producing dye. There is a small fort, El Tostón, and the nicest part of the town is around the old harbour where there is quite an eclectic selection of cafés and restaurants.

From El Cotillo, a road leads to the Faro del Cotillo, a lighthouse built in 1897 which is also home to Museo de la Pesca, a very detailed museum about the local fishing community (entrance €5). There are coastal paths leading to small sandy coves for those more interested in scenery than history.

El Cotillo to Lajares

Backtracking on the road to La Oliva, take the FV109 through Lajares which is a short cut back to the FV101 and Corralejo. Lajares is an odd, but likeable, small town thanks to the fact that it has a surf dude personality even though it's inland. There are some excellent cafés in the town serving food a bit different from the usual fare. Lajares is also a good spot for stretching the legs as a path leads right to the rim of Calderón Hondo, a volcanic crater. Apart from the views, it's a popular spot with the local Barbary squirrel population and one of the many diverse and interesting walking routes on Fuerteventura. From Lajares it's a straightforward drive back to Corralejo.

For more ideas for interesting activities on the amber Canary Island, take a look at our suggestions for 5 hot things to do on Fuerteventura in this book.

Driving on Fuerteventura, discovering the southern sights

Having previously explored the sand dune rich north of Fuerteventura by car, we turn the wheel in the direction of the south of the amber island where, as well as picturesque historic towns and gentle windmills, there are a few curios to seek out, including a lighthouse on the closest point to Africa in the Canary Islands.

This is our suggestion for a driving route around the south and centre of Fuerteventura.

Salinas del Carmen

Follow the FV2 south until, just beyond Caleta de Fuste, you reach Las Salinas del Carmen (open Tuesday to Saturday 10am-6pm, entrance €5). These salt pans have been providing the salty covering for papas arrugadas (the Canarian speciality wrinkled potatoes) since the 19th century and rows of neat white mounds create a startling contrast to the shallow orange pits. There is a Salt Museum attached which is relatively interesting, and a good place to pick up some Fuerteventura 'sal', but the best bit is to just stroll around the basins, hopefully witnessing a couple of 'salineros' at work. Other sights to see at Las Salinas are the skeleton of a whale and the occasional cheeky Barbary squirrel.

Faro de la Entallada

Continue south on the FV2, veering off on the FV4 towards Gran Tarajal and then the FV512 toward Las Playitas. Just before you reach the town, a narrow road leads to the part of the Canary Islands closest to Africa, the Faro de la Entallada. The final section of the road isn't for the faint-hearted as the single lane track climbs into hills and you pray there's no traffic coming the other way. But the rewards are worth the nervy journey. The lighthouse at the end of the road was built in 1954 and has played a role in guiding planes as well as ships. There's a decent car park (thankfully after the drive up) and a walkway leads out over the rocks, just in case you didn't think the views from the lighthouse were dramatic enough.

Mirador Risco de las Peñas

Return to the FV2 and cross over it, taking the FV20 to Tuineje and then the FV30 through Pajara to reach the Mirador Risco de las Peñas. The views are supposed to be the reason to stop here, but everyone knows it's the army of 'performing' Barbary squirrels who are the true draw. The signs say don't feed them... and nobody pays any attention. The cutest show on Fuerteventura.

Betancuria

Stay on the FV30 to arrive at Fuerteventura's most picturesque town, Betancuria. There's been a settlement in the area since 1404 when it's claimed Jean de Bethencourt founded the town, and former capital, after conquering the island. Now Betancuria's perfectly preserved, and flower-lined, historic streets welcome coachloads of visitors throughout the day.

Mirador Guise y Ayosa

Drive onwards and upwards into the hills above Betancuria to reach the Mirador Guise y Ayosa, easily spotted as there are two huge statues of the Mahoh kings the viewpoint is named after. These two ruled Fuerteventura before the conquistadors arrived to soil the party.

From the mirador stay on the FV30 until it becomes the FV20 and follow it all the way to Puerto del Rosario, the island's capital.

Puerto del Rosario is quite an unremarkable town, but it does have an obsession with sculptures. It's worth following the quirky sculpture trail there, breaking it up with some tapas in one of the bars near the centre of the town, before calling it a day and heading for home.

Five or more hot things to do on Fuerteventura

It's impossible to ignore the fact that Fuerteventura's greatest attraction is its beaches. The Canary Island boasts the sort of playas that automatically have the theme from Lawrence of Arabia going around your head... if you're old enough to remember it. Whilst it's impossible to ignore them, there are other qualities that give the second largest Canary Island a personality that sets it apart from the other islands.

Sunbathe au natural

I did say it was impossible to ignore the beaches. If you're going to go to Fuerteventura to perk up the tan, why not do it properly and not be left with a two-tone body for a change. If there's anywhere to strip off completely to soak up the sun, it's Fuerteventura.

The golden dunes around Corralejo and El Cotillo in the north and Jandia in the south are so expansive that even the most shy naturist should be able to find a discreet spot to expose all in complete privacy.

Plenty of sunseekers on these beaches aren't so coy. Try to take a photo of the gorgeous sands and you can be sure that somewhere in the frame there will be a man standing surveying the views, hands on hips, letting it all hang out.

You don't have to go all the way to enjoy Fuerteventura's gorgeous beaches. However, if others sunbathing naked is an issue, stick to the beaches closest to the resorts.

Eat cheese

With Fuerteventura's legendary weather and waves drawing surfers, windsurfers, kite-boarders and... err SUP-pers to the island, the obvious thing would be to suggest people take to the water. But jumping on a board is a niche activity that not everybody is either able, or particarly wants to do. We can all pop a chunk of cheese into our mouths though.

On Fuerteventura, goats rule. There are far more of them than human residents. The capital, Puerto del Rosario was once known as Puerto des Cabras Port of the Goats. The cheese from Fuerteventura is famous across the Canary Islands for being a savoury sensation. In fact it's renowned internationally, winning prestigious awards every year.

Known as Majorero, after the breed of goats it's produced from, it is sold as fresco (or tierno), semi-curado and curado. Fresco would suit people who don't like their cheese to have much of a personality. Semi-curado is matured for between 20 and 60 days and packs a decent, tangy punch. Curado is the choice for cheese die hards. Matured for over 60 days, it strains at its packaging to unleash its assertive flavours in your mouth.

For the more adventurous who'd like the full Fuerteventura cheesy experience, there's also goat milk liqueur. It's not as bad as it sounds, trust me, but I won't be replacing my stock of red vino with it.

Visit a goat farm to chalk up the lot and photograph some cute kids into the bargain.

Aloe vera

The volcanic curves of Fuerteventura's landscape is lacking in plant life, which makes endless fields of spiky aloe vera all the more surreal and surprising when you stumble across them. Aloe vera is one of the world's wonder plants and has been for aeons. Alexander the Great used it to heal battle wounds and Cleopatra slapped it on to make her more beautiful.

You can wash your hair with it, use it as shower gel, keep your skin young, use it as sun protection, spray it on as perfume and even drink it. It's claimed that Fuerteventura's climate is responsible for making the aloe vera grown there the best in the world.

A trip to an Aloe Vera factory isn't only a fascinating eye opener, you might come away looking years younger.

Salt Museum

The Salt Museum and Salinas del Carmen, close to Caleta de Fuste, consist of a museum dedicated to the history of salt and rows of neat white beds, the salinas. The museum is interesting, and you can pick up bags of salt in the attached shop, but maybe not something that makes you think 'wow, I've got to go there'. The salinas beside the museum are the real attraction.

The people of Fuerteventura have been working these salt basins since the late 19th century and they're the only working salinas left on the island. Miniature snowy white mountains of salt sharply contrast against burnt orange earth and ebony volcanic rocks to create a scene that is almost zen-like in its tranquil beauty. It is strangely soothing to explore the paths that dissect the salinas and fascinating to watch the old men 'rake' the salt.

A skeleton sculpture of a large whale between the salinas and the sea is an added bonus.

Barbary squirrel watching

Anyone who knows the Canary Islands will know that even though they are near Africa, there's a dearth of wildlife. The Barbary squirrel might not exactly be in the 'big five' league but when there's a lack of other animals, spotting one can be something to get quite excited about. Fuerteventura has lots of them.

We can kid ourselves that we head to the Mirador Risco de las Peñas, near Betancuria, to be overwhelmed by Fuerteventura's vibrant orange, volcanic scenery. But when the ardillas (Barbary squirrels) start hopping from rock to rock and striking up poses they've nicked from a meerkat documentary, the vistas are forgotten about. Their antics also serve to distract visitors from the signs advising 'Feeding or giving water to the fauna alters the balance of the colonies. Please avoid doing this.'

They are possibly the cutest sight you'll see on any Canary Island.

With quaint and pretty historic towns, unusual museums set in caves, lighthouses and windmills and a capital city with an obsession for sculptures to discover as well, it's worth dusting of the sand every so often and taking time to find out what makes Fuerteventura a quite special place to visit.

Golf on Fuerteventura

A Guide to Fuerteventura's Golf Courses.
Fuerteventura Golf Course
Golf is a very popular sport on Fuerteventura. The first golf course on the Island was created in Caleta de Fuste (Costa Caleta). This is a really excellent course, designed by Juan Catarineu, and which hosted the Spanish Open in 2004, which was quite an achievement for a course which only opened in Spring 2002.

Despite Fuerteventura's almost constant sunshine and little rain, the golf course has beautiful greens. The winds provide a challenge for all golfers. there are three lakes and other natural hazards.

The golf course also boasts a 5 star clubhouse, the Elba Palace Golf Resort Hotel, which homes the pro shop and the resident PGA professional. It has a driving range, chipping area, practice bunker and putting green. Practice facilities include a 50 bay driving range, club and buggy hire, a large putting green and a second green for chipping and bunker shots.

This course is designed around luxurious villa complexes many of these villas being available for rental.

Las Salinas Golf Course.
The second course to open was built alongside the first one in Caleta. This is very well set up as a course that is ideal for the holidaymaker type golfer, as well as experienced golfer, it being slightly less challenging than Fuerteventura Golf Course. This course is currently maintained in very good condition.

It is a par 70 course designed for Manolo Piñeiro, twice world champion golfer. The course´s amenities amenities include a club house, pro shop, buggy, trolley and club hire, a cafeteria, restaurant and changing rooms with showers and lockers.

Las Playitas Golf Course.
In 2010 the Golf course of Las Playitas opened the further nine holes required to make it a full golf course. There is a driving range, for

around 30 golfers. It is a very well planned and challenging course. The pro here is British PGA professional Murdo McCorquodale, who speaks English, Spanish and German. The Golf Course at Las Playitas Golf course is just a few kilometres away from Gran Tarajal.

Corralejo Golf course.
There is a 9 hole course on the Parque Natural development in the south of Corralejo, and it´s called the Mirador de Lobos Golf. It´s a 673m course, with a practise net area and putting/chipping greens.

All in all Fuerteventura is developing into an ideal destination for those who like a little golf on holiday and for those that want an entire holiday designed around that theme.

Jandia Golf Course (Closed at the moment - Oct 2011).
The course in Jandia, on the right as you enter Morro Jable, though open still has a few teething problems. The course is quite hilly and would be more suitable if the course had buggiess, but at the moment there aren't any. The paths between tees aren't clearly defined and it can be difficult to find the next tee. It is well laid out and if the teething problems can be sorted out this promises to be a good course.

Thanks to Mr and Mrs Jones from arround Bicester for providing us with some information for this page. We met them at the Jandia Golf course and we were pleased that they were Sunnyfuerteventura.com fans.

Work on that swing of yours on Fuerteventura's golf courses

Fuerteventura makes for a great golfing destination. Not least because rain rarely stops play. Here's a handy guide to the island's golf courses, including contact details, distance from airport and resort+, and green fees.

1.) Fuerteventura Golf Club

Temperatures don't dip much below 23 degrees Centigrade on this Atlantic-side 18-holer. As well as a par-72 course, there's 800 square metres of putting green and a driving range which can hold up to 50 people. There's also a chipping green at the Fuerteventura Golf Club.

Designed by architect Juan Caterineu, FGC opened as Fuerteventura's first-ever course back in 2002. Two years later, it hosted the Spanish Open. No matter what language you speak, you'll receive tuition at the Fuerteventura Golf Club's Golf School in your native tongue.

Contact details: Calle del Golf 1, Urbanizacion Fuerteventura Golf Club, 35610, Caleta de Fuste, Antigua. (+34) 928 160 034.

Distance from airport: 10.7km (6.6 miles)

Distance from Corralejo: 48.2km (30 miles)

Distance from Puerto del Rosario: 16km (9.9 miles)

Green fees: 75€

2.) Jandia Golf Course

Located close to Fuerteventura's southerly resorts, Jandia Golf Course's layout was the brainchild of legendary architect, Ron Kirby. Designed to be a blend of fun and a challenge, it's a par-72 course. 5,900 metres in length, its shaded driving range can accommodate up to 20 golfers.

You'll find Jandia Golf's clubhouse located in the centre of the course. It's home to a Pro Shop, as well as buggy & club rental, and locker rooms. Sensitively built on a stunning valley, you might well be treated to a glimpse of the local wildlife who have maintained their home here.

Contact details: Barranco Vinamar S/N, 35625, Morro Jable. (+34) 928 871 979.

Distance from airport: 81.8km (50.8 miles)

Distance from Corralejo: 119km (73.9 miles)

Distance from Puerto del Rosario: 87km (54.1 miles)

Green fees: 70€

3.) Mirador de Lobos Golf Club

Hit the north of the island to visit Mirador de Lobos Golf Club which forms part of the Parque Natural de Corralejo. This par-3 nine-hole pitch and putt becomes an 18-hole course with the use of flags to change the route the golf party follows. Making it suitable for absolute beginners up to expert pros.

Enjoy fantastic Atlantic views as well as vistas of Corralejo's out-of-this-world dunes. Beautifully tended, the Mirador de Lobos Golf Club stands out as a green oasis in northern Fuerteventura's desert setting. Marvel at how lush the fairways, green, and even rough are.

Contact details: Calle Tarabilla 1, 35640, Corralejo. (+34) 928 854 789.
Distance from airport: 40.7km (25.3 miles)
Distance from Corralejo: 4.1km (2.5 miles)
Distance from Puerto del Rosario: 33.4km (20.8 miles)
Green fees: 20€

4.) Playitas Golf

The climate may well be tropical, but the atmosphere at Playitas Golf feels positively Home Counties. Especially with the strict adherence to clothing. No beachwear's allowed and golfers must wear polo shirts, golf shoes, or trainers whether playing or practising.

This par-67 18-hole course extends to a distance of 4,824 metres. Scottish golf-course architect John Chilver Stainer's the creative genius behind its challenging contours. There are four ponds and other water features to contend with, although your biggest obstacle might well be a natural one. Namely, the wind.

Contact details: Urbanizacion Las Playitas, 35629, Tuineje. (+34) 928 860 400.

Distance from airport: 43.6km (27.1 miles)

Distance from Corralejo: 81km (50.3 miles)

Distance from Puerto del Rosario: 48.9km (30.4 miles)

Green fees: 64€

5.) Golf Club Salinas de Antigua

Fuerteventura's eternal spring means that you can play Golf Club Salinas de Antigua all year round without worrying about the weather. Two-time golfing world champion Manolo Pinero designed the par-70 18-hole course. Male golfers will have to navigate a maximum of 5,409 metres whilst their female counterparts face up to 4,652 metres.

Extensive facilities include golf shop, restaurant, and cafeteria. Golf Club Salinas de Antigua's also home to changing rooms, showers, and golf-club rental. The club's resident pro is available to hire, providing lessons for players of all levels.

Contact details: Carretera Jandia Km 12, 35610, Antigua. (+34) 928 877 272.

Distance from airport: 11.2km (7 miles)

Distance from Corralejo: 48.6km (30.2 miles)

Distance from Puerto del Rosario: 16.4km (10.2 miles)

Green fees: 75€

Morro Jable, Fuerteventura

Morro Jable is at the southern end of Fuerteventura, just under one hours drive south of the airport. A new section of road was opened in September 2005 and this reduced the transfer times by about ten minutes, as the new road is both straight and level, and replaces a narrower windier coastal road in Jandia.

If you find yourself out for a drive in a hire car it is worth taking the more scenic route as it allows the driver to take in the views, while still concentrating on the road.

Morro Jable, Old and New
The older parts of Morro Jable are either side of the headland around which the village was built. The port was originally the home of the fishing fleet, and still is, but now hosts a variety of tourist attractions, including a catamaran and several sports fishing vessels, and a ferry service to Gran Canaria.

The part of the old village that is separated from the port by the headland runs up a barranco, or valley, into the hills. The newer parts of the town have been built to connect the old village area and the port area, and the tourist facilities have been built along the coast to the east of the old village, in such a way that Morro Jable now stretches for a mile or so along the coast, the newer parts having been appended to the older parts in a pleasant way.

Tourism in Morro Jable
Most of the tourists that visit Morro Jable are German and this is reflected in the higher percentage of German restaurant and bar owners. The newer part of the town has been built along the beachfront to the east of the port. The promenade at Morro Jable makes up the main part of the newer town and there are numerous shops, restaurants and bars, all with views towards the sea.

The beach at Morro Jable is part of a long line of natural white sandy beaches. The beach to the east (left as you look to sea) of the impressive lighthouse is used more by naturists, while that to the west is used more by non naturists. On the beach to the west of the lighthouse it is possible to hire yachts to sail.

All the facilities that you would expect to find in a beach resort, that is close to seas abundant with life, can be found in the resort.

Tourist Information
The tourist Information office can now be found alongside where the market is held, under the shopping centre

Cofete, Fuerteventura

Cofete is located on the Barlovento (windward) coast of Jandia. To get there you have to travel over 20 kilometres of track, that only allows for single file traffic in some places. Some of these places have steep drops to the side, amd the journey is best done in a jeep or four wheel drive vehicle.

Having said that some of the views are magnificent, and Cofete beach is about 5 kilometres in length, and is also one of the wider beaches on the island. This makes it a worthwhile trip, if you are looking to appreciate the space that Fuerteventura has to offer.

To reach Cofete, you must take the road from Morro Jable. This road is signposted to Cofete, and turns into a track after a couple of kilometres. After about 10 kilometres, there is a fork in the road, and a car park and road sign, and you need to turn right. The track winds up and over the hills and one of the best views on the island is to be had just before you begin the descent. There is a viewing platform there.

One interesting feature of the decent, is the abundance of one particular species of cactus (cacti standyupiie, you can see we are not botanists!), which we haven't seen growing anywhere else, certainly not in the same abundance.

As we drove down the descent, we noticed a group on intrepid cyclists heading the other way, so we pulled into a passing place so that we could take their photographs. The lead rider said something friendly in German. Most of the tourists down here are German, and all the football flags in the bar at Cofete are for German teams.

If you do go in a car, you would be as well parking at the restaurant, the short length of track between there and the beach is particularly bumpy.

There are a couple of things of interest, as well as the beach. There is a cemetery (we are working on the significance of the cemetery). Villa Winter, which originally belonged to a mysterious German named Gustav Winter. There are all kinds of rumours about this gentleman. He is rumoured to have had links with General Franco, the German wartime leaders, and a secret submarine base. It would have certainly suited Greta Garbo to live in the villa.

The villa has Mount Jandia, the highest point on the island, as an impressive backdrop. One of the reasons that Fuerteventura is drier than Tenerife and Gran Canaria, is that only mountains above 800 metres will cause precipitation. Mount Jandia is the only peak above 800 metres on the island. The changing cloud formation around Mount Jandia means that the scenery is contantly changing as the quality of the light is affected by clouds

Puerto del Rosario, Fuerteventura

Puerto del Rosario is the capital of Fuerteventura, and has around 40,000 inhabitants. It is based around a port that has grown from its humble origins as the Puerto del Cabras (port of the goats) into a busy working port that continues to develop. There has been recent improvements so that large cruise ships can dock and also Playa Chica, the local beach has recently been improved by making it triple the original size, for the benefit of residents and the visitors from the cruise ships.

Until recently, little of the activity in the capital of Fuerteventura was based on tourism, but this is slowly changing as the Cabildo and other governmental bodies are actively seeking to raise the capitals profile in terms of tourism. A tourist information office, in the form of a kiosk, was opened on the "promenade", close to the harbour. The entire sea front in Puerto del Rosario continues to be developed and improved.

Puerto del Rosario is easily visited from other parts of the island as buses run to Puerto del Rosario from all the major towns on Fuerteventura. A bus journey to Puerto del Rosario to Caleta de Fuste takes around 20 minutes and to Corralejo about 40, with services to and from both, every half an hour. The bus station was opened in 2008, and from there you can get a bus all around the island.

If you are considering a shopping trip it is worth bearing in mind that lots of the shops close for the siesta. However, the Las Rotundas Shopping Centre is open from 10am - 10 pm from Monday to Saturday (closed Sunday). It is located on the south side of the town next to the main road which links Puerto del Rosario and the airport. The main entrance is next to the Sundial roundabout. The shopping centre 2 levels of underground car parking (free parking), and four floors of commercial businesses with around 100 units There is a large supermarket, with shops of adult fashion, children's fashion, shoes, jewellers, beauty, leisure and sports, electrical and mobile phones etc. There are several cafes and restaurants too, and a Burger King on the top floor.

The main public buildings and church are located around the pedestrianised Primero de Mayo street, which is becoming increasingly popular now that it has been pedestrionised with serveral street cafes.

An increasing number of cruise ships are stopping in the capital on Canary Islands tours during the winter months and in the summer too.

Puerto del Rosario is a good place to practise speaking Spanish and allows an insight into the daily life of Fuerteventurans, or at least those that live in this "city". The Fuerteventuran accent is quite different to the standard Spanish that is used on language course tapes, but if you are talking about food and cerveza, it is not too difficult to follow.

One interesting feature of the capital is the statues that are to be found around the town. These form part of an open air exhibition and many have been produced during competitions that are held in the capital. A booklet, Puerto del Rosario on Foot, is available at the tourist office, and gives a guided route around the town.

Carnival time is important to the residents of Puerto del Rosario and the spring celebrations are held in mid February

Fairly recently the Palacio de Formacion Congresos has opened which has an auditorium where attractions such as the Moscow Ballet's performance of Swan Lake can be seen during their winter tour

1915/16. There is also an ice show called Alegria held near the bus station over this Christmas.

Here is a guide to some of the fiestas on the island, but these are subject to change.

Fiestas

Place	Fiesta of	Date
Puerto del Rosario	Nuestra senora del Rosario	7th October
Ampuyenta	San Pedro Alcantara	19th October
Castillas del Angel	Santa Ana	26th July
El Matorral	San Juan	24th June
El Time	Nuestra Senora de la Merced	24th September
Guisguey	San Pedro	29th June
La Asomada	Nuestra Senora de Fatima	13th May
La Matilla	Nuestra Senora del Sirocco	7th August
Llanos de la Concepcion	Nuestra Senora de la Concepcion	15th August
Los Estancos	Santa Rita	23rd May
Puerto Lajas	Procession of Nuestra Senora del Pino	12th October
Tefia	Santa Monica	4th May
	San Agustin	28th August

Tetir	Santo Domingo	4th August
	San Andres	30th November
Las Parcelas	San Andres	1st Sunday in December

Ajuy, Fuerteventura

Ajuy is a small village on the West coast of Fuerteventura. It is less than a twenty minute drive from Pajara, most of the drive is along the valley which has Ajuy at its mouth.

The beach at Ajuy is attractive, though covered with black sand. A couple of the few restaurants in the village are on or close to the beach.

The village is probably most visited because of the caves that are to be found a short walk from the town. The path to the caves is to be found at the northern end of the beach, and leads past the hut that has been built into the rock face.

The views from the path are quite impressive, as the coast in this area consists mainly of cliffs.

The caves are quite impressive, and can be entered via a series of steps that have to be navigated with care. We are not sure that it is sensible to enter the caves without some sort of protective head gear that a speliologist would wear as a matter of course.

Corralejo Fuerteventura

Corralejo is a tourist resort situated at the northern end of Fuerteventura. It is considerably larger than Caleta de Fuste and has a more touristy feel.

Corralejo Old Town

The original part of the town is based around the old harbour, which was used by local fishermen. Here the small sheltered beach, Playa la Clavellina, provides safe bathing for locals and holidaymakers alike. Fishing from the harbour wall is a popular pastime, and it is not usually as busy as the photograph suggests. On this particular day there was a competitive swim from Lobos back to Corralejo, and people who had been visiting the tourist information office, as well as relatives of those taking part crowded onto the wall for a good view.

Corralejo Marina

The more modern facility consists of a marina for pleasure craft and room for the ferry services to Lanzarote and Lobos, a small island that is a 15 minute ferry ride from Fuerteventura. There are various trips aimed at those on holiday that run from the harbour, and bookings for these can be made at one of the booths dotted about the area.

Corralejo Market

The market is held on Tuesdays and Fridays close to the Baku water park.It starts about 9.30 and finishes about 1.30 depending on how busy it is. Here you will find a lot of crafts as people living on the island will turn their hand to anything that can make them a living. As well as clothes, shoes and household goods and souvenirs there is also a range of interesting African wooden crafts and artwork on sale. Why not haggle the price and get yourself a real bargain!

Corralejo's Beaches and Dunes

A short distance south of the old port are a couple of more spacious sandy beaches that have fine views of the Island of Lobos. Whereas the small beach by the old harbour in Corralejo seems to making use of the space, these larger beaches are aimed at holidaymakers staying in the north of Fuerteventura, and have everything needed for a day at the beach on Fuerteventura.

The town is surrounded by sand dunes and miles of sandy beaches that form a nature reserve. The beaches between Punta de Tivas and the Tres Islas hotels, called Playa del Pozo, Playa del Medano and

Playa de Viejo run in to each other and this sandy shore is sometimes called Flag Beach. These beaches are exposed to the wind and this makes these beaches ideal places to pursue those activities that require a little more life to the water. Circular stone structures provide a windbreak for those that just want to take advantage of Fuerteventura's sunny climate.

Some of these beaches, though it is really one long beach, are used by naturists. The attitude to naturism on Fuerteventura is relaxed and as such there are no designated naturist beaches. Naturists generally prefer to be on beaches that are away from the resort centres, so that they don't offend other bathers. The beach at Playa de Pozo seems to be the most popular with naturists.

Getting to Corralejo

Transfer times from Fuerteventura airport to the holiday accommodation in Corralejo is about 4o minutes. You could also travel by bus, guagua, as they are known in Spanish. This would involve taking a ten minute journey into Puerto del Rosario on the number 3, then the number 6 bus to Corralejo. The journey is quite pleasant, going through some interesting villages. As you get close to Corralejo to your left you will see the Caderilla de Roja, which is one of the extinct volcanoes that created these islands, and to the right some lovely sandy beaches that stretch up most of the coast to Corralejo. If you are staying in El Cotillo, you can catch the number 8 bus from Corralejo, or the number 7 from Puerto del Rosario.

Sport in and around Corralejo

Corralejo´s location on Fuerteventura means that it is well positioned for many sports activities. There are north and east facing beaches close by and this allows those who enjoy surfing, windsurfing or kite boarding to move to spend their days in different locations depending upon how the wind is affecting the waves or blowing in relation to the shore.

Those that are into hiking or mountain biking have a choice of off road tracks and the distances travelled can be adjusted to suit the time available.

Adventurous tours.

Besides trike tours, there are other possibilities including Buggy Tours and excursions as well as quad bike tours, and all of these prove popular with holidaymakers

Costa Calma, Fuerteventura

Costa Calma is a true beach resort, having been built adjacent to a mile long section at the start of the white sandy beaches that run for about twelve miles from Costa Calma to Morro Jable. The colourful seas that lap the shores of this part of Fuerteventura are relatively benign and the area as a whole is very popular with beach lovers and wind surfers.

Costa Calma Hotels

The beach-front part of the resort runs from the Hotel Rio Calma, a very swish affair, with its own waterfall, fresh water pool at the edge of the sea, and opulent gardens, to the Hotel Esmerelda, which though a little less secluded has the benefit of being closer to the wind surf schools and other activity centres of Costa Calma.

The sea front between these two hotels has a range of other hotels and aparthotels with various star or key ratings that allow easy access to the shore. None of the hotels that are not on the shoreline are a great distance from the sea and their slightly elevated position gives then good views of Costa Calma and the surrounding dunes.

Costa Calma's development.

Costa Calma was built around a small village called Cañada Del Rio, though it is now difficult to see how the original pueblo fitted into the landscape. The attraction for the tourism industry was the sandy beaches, but care was taken when the resort was being developed to make sure that countryside did not disappear under concrete. The built up areas of Costa Calma are separated from each other by a green zone that runs the length of the resort. This provides a haven for wildlife, and we spotted several European Hoopoes. This greenbelt provides a pleasant area to walk through during the day, but on a dark night it is a little spooky. It does not take too much imagination to feel that any second the trees are likely to talk to you.

A new paved walkway has been buit between the greenbelt and the main road, and this links the shopping centre and development at the south of the village to the centre. It is also lit up at night.

The length of the resort means that it is no real central area to Costa Calma, but there are several small shopping centres with restaurants and shops that act as a nucleus for the immediate vicinty.

One of the events in Costa Calma that does act as a focal point is the Sunday morning market. This is a colourful, crowded affair that starts about 9 and carries on until early afternoon. The whole range of goods that you would expect to find on a holiday island is available from the stallholders who represent numerous nationalites.

Costa Calma Beach

The beach at Costa Calma, which is cleaned daily, is long enough for early morning joggers to have a decent workout by running the length of it a couple of times.

Early each morning joggers, nordic walkers (nordic walking involves the use of poles similar to those used by skiers) and swimmers can be seen taking their morning excercise. Later in the day the beach at Costa Calma has more of a relaxed feel to it as the sunbathers relax in the sunshine.

The tourists in Costa Calma seem to be largely German. This is evident in that when we bought a drink in a bar the cost was often quoted in German. Many of the cafes emphasize their German ownership, and the entertainment tends to be in German rather than English.

El Cotillo, Fuerteventura

El Cotillo is a small fishing village at the northern end of Fuerteventura, on the west coast. The village is centred around the small harbour that is mostly used by local fishermen. The harbour where the boats are to be found is actually relatively new. The old harbour is only a short walk to the north over the headland that separates the two. There are several bars and restaurants close to the old harbour.

El Cotillo's history.
As it is in a quiet spot on the island you can understand its history as a smuggler's village. The tower was built around 1741 after repeated attacks by English pirates. The tower is known as EL Toston and also in

Spanish by Castillo de Rico Roque, and was built for the commandante Andres Bonito. The tower is open to tourists and often hosts exhibitions such as paintings.

El Cotillo Beaches

There are miles of beaches to the south of this part of sunny Fuerteventura. The beaches are excellent, and even on a busy day they are too big to be overcrowded. To the north are the lagoon beaches of shallow clear water and white sand contrasting against the black volcanic rock. The biggest of the beaches, La Concha, has a large car park, a beach bar and a lovely beach. It gets very busy with locals and tourists. The smaller lagoon beaches are favourite places for naturists. There are more lagoon beaches to the east of the lighthouse.

A couple of miles to the north of El Cotillo there is a lighthouse which is also a fishing museum, and a pleasant afternoon can be spent wandering there and back.

Getting to El Cotillo

El Cotillo is easily reached by public transport. It is a short journey from Corralejo, take the number 8 bus. The number 7 route, from Puerto del Rosario to El Cotillo, crosses Fuerteventura and rewards the traveller with some excellent views. Timetables can be found by following the link to the getting about page which has a link directly to bus timetables.

If you are going to El Cotillo by car, then there is a very picturesque drive along the coast, see details below:

Corralejo to El Cotillo by Car
This tour takes about 3 hours, the condition of the track means that it is just about passable in a car. It would be better to make the trip in a vehicle with a bit of ground clearance.

The track begins close to the bus station in Corralejo and ends close to the lighthouse at El Cotillo. From there the track back to the village of El Cotillo is easily navigated.

At the start of the journey, Lanzarote is clearly visible, and as seems to be usual, we saw a ferry heading off somewhere via the west coast of Fuerteventura.

The distance covered is about fifteen miles and there are only two or three small settlements and a few isolated houses along the route. There is a development called Origo Mare being built close to Majanicho, which will no doubt make this route busier when it is completed.

It is probably a good idea to take drinks with you as we did not find anywhere to buy things along the way.

Soon we arrived at Majanicho, a little village situated on the edge of a large bay. It is well worth a visit. The chapel there is very pretty and typical of those on the island. The bay looks very shallow and well protected and is therefore and ideal spot for a fishing village. There are pretty views across the bay.

Further alont the track we came to an almost desterted beach, except for a couple from London who were playing bat and ball. There is nothing like that sight to remind me of the cold summer holidays of my childhood in England!

The length of the northern coast is popular with surfers and those looking for an isolated sunbathing spot. We took several photographs of the surfers along the route

When the lighthouse, Faro de Toston came into view we spotted the windsurfer, and stopped for a while to watch and take more photographs.

The road from the lighthouse is a better road, leading to El Cotillo. There we have an interesting spectacle of tarmacced wide roads that go nowhere in particular.

On arriving in El Cotillo we visited the El Toston bar for a well deserved drink and a lovely salad each.

Costa Caleta, Fuerteventura

A safe family holiday resort.
Caleta de Fuste is a purpose built holiday resort, with safe beaches for the family. Although there is no old town area there are some old fortifications by the Atlantic shopping centre and at the other end of the beach near the harbour. Caleta was created around the original cove, which developed into a harbour and beach resort because it offered safe sheltered environment.

The Beaches at Caleta

The beaches at Caleta continue to be improved and the final works are close to completion. Originally there was one large beach in Caleta, created by importing some pale golden sand making it perfect for sunbathing and swimming. This beach area had recently undergone improvements with the addition of new toilet facilities, the removal of stones that had washed up over time, and the creation of a café directly on the original beach. Later further new beaches were towards the Atlantico Shopping centre to improve facilities for the Hotel Sara, Sheraton and Elba Carlotta Hotels.

These beaches were made by creating lagoons out of the solid rock, then importing sand to make a beach. There is a restaurant here out in the sea accessed via a walkway. It is called the Chiringuito. This beach is nice if you want a quick sunbathe before doing your shopping. Again it is quite safe, as these bathing areas are mainly surrounded by rock. The most recent beach works are almost completed, improving the area between Caleta and the Atlantico centre, opposite Gone Fishing and the Beach Cafe.

There are around three dozen holiday complexes around Caleta de Fuste, most offering one or two bed apartments, self catering facilities, centred around a pool.

The apartment complexes are in three main areas, the central town of Caleta de Fuste, Costa Antigua, to the north, and Chipmunk mountain to the east (its not really a mountain, but it is uphill). There are lots of hotels and restaurants to choose from and they are generally of a very high standard.

Jandia, Fuerteventura

Jandia is the peninsula at the southern end of Fuerteventura. It includes the resorts of Costa Calma and Playas de Jandia, as well as the port of Morro Jable and several smaller resorts. The highest point on

Fuerteventura, Pico de Zarza, is to be found there, and once upon a time Jandia was separated from the rest of Fuerteventura by the sea. The deposits of sand that linked the two have resulted in some of the bestbeaches in the world.

Travelling to Jandia

All the civilised parts of Jandia can be reached in less than an hour from Fuerteventura airport. It used to take a little over an hour to reach Morro Jable, but the opening the new motorway a few years ago has reduced the journey time from the north of Fuerteventura to Morro Jable by around ten minutes.

Jandia Bars and Restaurants

Most of the tourists that stay in Jandia are German and this is reflected in the higher percentage of German owned restaurants and bars. There are lots of Spanish owned bars and restaurants and one or two British owned bars, as well as a few belonging to other nationalities.

Playas de Jandia

The people of Pajara are rightly proud of the beaches of Jandia. The lighthouse at the Playa Del Matorral acts not only as a warning to shipping, but as the point at which the beach is divided into naturist and non naturist sections. On the beach to the north are more naturists, while that to the south is used more by non naturists.

The Playa de Sotavento (leeward beach) is in the lee of the wind. There is a very long spit here and an enormous "lake" appears at high tide. The Reni Egli centre is to be found here and the are always windsurfers and kite boarders practising their art here.

The Playa De Barlovento (windward beach) and the Playa de Cofete are much less accessible, and the sea conditions here are much wilder. An excellent view of both can be seen from the Pico de Zarza.

The wilder parts of the island that are to be found beyond Morro Jable are well worth a visit, but we would recommend the use of a 4 wheel drive or Jeep to reach them.

Antigua, Fuerteventura

Antigua is a small town, but it is the administrative centre for the municipality of Antigua. Most of the municipality of Antigua covers a plain some 200 metres above sea level and this made it ideal, in the past, for the location of windmills. The towns and villages of Agua de Bueyes, Casillas Morales, Valles de Ortega, La Corte, Antigua, Las Pocetas, Los Alares, Pozo Negro, Las Salinas del Carmen, Caleta de Fustes, Costa de Antigua, Los Llanoz del dinerro and Triquvijate are all located within the municipality. Many of these hold fiestas, (see below for details).

The Centro de Artesania, a tourist attraction based around a restored windmill, can be found in the town of Antigua. Besides the restored windmill, that allows visitors to see the inside of a restored windmill there is a fine cactus garden, a restaurant and several craft workshops.

The church of Iglesia de Nuestra Señora de Antigua, originally built in 1785, and restored in the last century, is very picturesque. When we visited Antigua, the church was open to the public, as is often the case. The inside of the church is worth seeing.

The address of the ayuntamiento, or town hall is C/Marcos Trujillo no1, Antigua. Tel 928878004/928 878105

Fiestas		
Place	Fiesta of	Date
Los Alares	Ntra. Sra. del Cobre	3rd Sunday in May
Triquivijate	San Isidro labrador	15th May and 2nd Sunday in August
Las Salinas	Ntra. Sra. del Carmen	16th July
Triquivijate	San Isidro labrador	15th May and 2nd Sunday in August
Valles de Ortega	San Roque	16th August

Las Pocetas	San Francisco Javier	27th August
Antigua	Ntra Sra de Antigua	8th September
Agua de Buyes	Ntra. Sra de Guadalupe	2nd Sunday in September
Casillas De Morales	Fiesta de los Peregrinos	Last Sunday in September
Caleta de Fuste	Virgen de la Pena del Mar	12th October

Costa Antigua, Fuerteventura

Costa Antigua is situated on the east coast of Fuerteventura, close to Caleta de Fuste , and only a short distance from Fuerteventura airport. The area is very "up and coming" and has improved a great deal recently, mostly due to pressure from the Neighbourhood Association on local polititians. The area was originally developed with tourism in mind, Caleta Paraiso and Cocosol being two of the more established complexes, which are now privately owned having been built as holiday complexes. The hotels that are in Costa Antigua,are the Costa Tropical and the Elba Lucia.

The visitors that appreciate Costa Antigua most are those that are looking for a relaxing break, a short distance away from the more touristy town of Caleta, it is very friendly as there is a community of residents, rather than just tourists. However, these days Costa Antigua is fast becoming the place to be!

Situated across the road from the Caleta Paraiso complex is Stoners restaurant and bar and the Crazy Goat Bar, which does great Karaoke evenings. There is also the Volvoretta bar that does cocktails and a wonderful meat platter meal if you book the day before. Well worth a try.

In the Antigua Bay complex, a little further towards the sea, there is Mustang Sallys, an Irish/American bar, where you can get good food, sports and live entertainment. If you are interested in playing golf then it has "links" to the Golf course. You may be able to borrow some clubs too!

You can also find Benny's bar which is a great spot to watch sports or to pick up a pizza. It is open from midday to late. On the other side of Benny's bar is a Chinese restaurant Jingsing, and further down is a Spanish bar called El Tamboril, that specialises in tapas. There is a new restaurant too named Kwizeen which does a range of high quality food, although I haven't yet tried it.

Just round the corner from Benny's International bar is the Bubbles Laundry and the Hire Hardware shop. The Costa Tropical hotel has a restaurant names Los Remos and also a pizzeria, Mama Mia and a beauty shop named Perfect Beauty where you can get a massage or your nails done etc.

There has been a lot of development going on in the area but this is coming to an end with villas being near to completion.

If you want to get to Caleta there is an attractive coastal walk that is populated by amusing chipmunks, that you can hand feed. This walkway has street lighting and which makes walking into or out of Costa Caleta after sundown a reasonable option. For those of you that regard walking as something not to be done on holiday, Caleta can also be reached by taxi. The fare is around 5 euros. You may also take the free bus courtesy of the Elba hotel, but this is dependent on the mood of the driver!

This leaves the Castillo Elba at 10.20,11.20,12.20,15.20,17.20,18.20 and 20.20, and arrives at the Atlantico Shopping Centre 15 minutes later, after going to the Hotel Sara, at the golf course. The bus leaves the Atlantico at 10.55, 11.55, 14.55, 16.55, 17.55 and 19.55, and arrives in Costa Antigua 20 minutes later, via the other Elba hotels in Caleta. the bus is primarily for residents of the Elba hotels but it is used by other residents too. There is generally no problem, but its best to tip the driver a few coins.

You can also walk the other way towards the airport where there is a little beach if perhaps you like the solitude.

Caleta Paraiso, Costa Antigua, Fuerteventura.

Caleta paraiso is located in Costa Antigua. This is a short walk from Caleta de Fuste, and is close to the airport. However although it is so close there is very little disturbance from planes as the do no fly directly overhead.

Most of the properties on the complex are one bedroom apartments on either ground or first floor. Some overlook the pool and bar area, others have views towards the sea.

The apartments have a bedroom, bathroom and a room with a kitchen/lounge area. They were initially designed to sleep three, but it is possible to sleep four in some apartments and still be friends at the end of the holiday.

There are also studios which consist of one room and a bathroom.

In either case some have been refurbished to a very high standard. All the apartments and studios have an outside patio area.

There are two pools that are sheltered from the prevailing wind to inprove the sunbathing experience. One of the pools is shallower than the other. There is a childrens' play area with sand, and a variety of climbing frames etc

There are supermarkets in the Costa Antigua area, a cashpoint, several restaurants and bars, Spanish and English and a launderette and a tool and cycle hire shop

Giniginamar, Fuerteventura

Giniginamar is a very attractive village set at the end of the valley of Giniginamar. The photograph was taken from the top of the hill at the western end of the south facing bay. There are a couple of bars that serve food in the village, and as you would expect in a small fishing village, fish is a particular speciality.

Also on the main street there is a quite modern style church of Nuestra Snra del Carmen, built in 1992, which has a lovely interior and modern stain glass windows. When we visited the church doors were being painted, we think because the fiesta of Nuestra Senora del Carmen, which is held on July 16th, the day after we visited.

There is a large beach area here, however the beach consists of pebbles rather than sand making it a pleasant experience for those not wanting to deposit large amounts of sand in their homes on returning from the beach!. The bathing apears to be quite safe, with a gentle slope out to the sea. Giniginamar bay is a protected zone because of its high biological interest.

The village also has a multiple sports court

Gran Tarajal, Fuerteventura

Gran Tarajal is the largest town in the municipality of Tuineje. It is built at the mouth of the Rio Gran Tarajal, but don't expect to find any water flowing for most of the year. There is a new harbour that has fishing and sports facilities and it is the home of an annual deep sea fishing contest, an international event that is held each Septemeber.

Gran Tarajal beach: There is an expansive beach at Gran Tarajal, that consists of a fine black sand. The bathing seems to be safe, and showers are provided at points on the promenade which adjoins the beach. We recommend you use these as the black sand seems to stick to your body more readily than the other varieties we have lain in.

The town: Being built at the mouth of a river, that has carved its way through the cliffs, many of the streets in Gran Tarajal are quite steep. They are also narrow and work is ongoing to improve the flow of traffic. The many bars and restaurants are predominantly owned by Canarians.

Shopping: Gran Tarajal has a large range of shops, but being a mainly Spanish town these tend to be closed in the early afternoon, for the siesta. We assume you can buy anything you need in Gran Tarajal but as we went purely for the sunbathing, we can't be sure!

Property Developments: Close to the harbour area there is a large new housing development being created

Lajares, Fuerteventura

Lajares is quite a trendy place, popular with surfing type young people. It is a fair sized village, that lies 6-8 kilometres from El Cotillo, Corralejo and La Oliva. The fact that it is quite spread out gives the impression, when you drive through it, that it is not as large as it actually is.

Facilities: The village has its own supermarket, cash machine and cake shop. Besides these there are some interesting shops, restaurants and bars. The shops include Artesania Lajares an artisan shop that sells a wide variety of Canarian craftwork. Lots of the other shops are related to watersports activities, and some of the islands best known bars and restaurants are to be found in the village.

Architecture: The village has an example of both a molino and a molina, which are actually just a few yards apart. These are both to be found near to the ermita de San Antonio (St Anthony's Chapel).

Getting There: If you are staying in Corralejo and are into walking, it is possible to walk to Lajares, along a route along the chain of volcanoes that run between the two.

Lajares is served by the buses that run between Corralejo and El Cotillo and Puerto del Rosario and El Cotillo, for bus timetables visit the getting about page. If you have hired a car it is certainly worth paying a visit to Lajares.

Artisan Market: Lajares has quite a large artisan market, held each Saturday until around 6pm. It was just before 6pm when we visited so it was rather quiet, but it gets quite busy earlier on and you can buy some unique craft items.

La Oliva, Fuerteventura

La Oliva is the main town of the municipality of the same name. The main towns of the municipality are Corralejo, El Cotillo, Parque Holandés, La Caldereta, Lajares, El Roque, Tindaya, Vallebron and Villaverde.

The address of the ayuntamuento in La Oliva is C/ Emilio Castellot, 2 La Oliva. Other municiple information is available on the municipal information page. The ayuntamiento is based in a modern building and we have always found the staff to be helpful and friendly.

The parish church of La Oliva, is dedicated to the Virgen de la Candelaria, has three naves and a tower of black stone.

Another building of note in the town is La Casa de los Coroneles. The building was restored and opened by the King and Queen of Spain in 2006, and is well worth a visit, and it is located just down from the ayuntamiento. It was built in 1708 and was the home of the military rulers of the island. The building usually has a mix of exhibitions on display, which change at different times of the year. It´s open from Tuesday - Sunday from 10am - 2pm and 4.30pm - 7pm. Entrance is free.

There are two other museums in the town, Museo Casa del Grano "la Cilla", which is open 10.00 - 17.00 (closed Mondays) and the Centro de Arte Canario, Casa Mane, which is also open from 10.00 - 17.00 (closed Sundays)

Municipalities of Fuerteventura

The island of Fuerteventura is divided into six municipalities; Antigua, Betancuria, Pajara, Tuineje, La Oliva and Puerto del Rosario. Each of these municipalities has its own character and culture, and some taxes are set by the municipalites. Each has a town hall, where such things as taxes need to be paid. For more information follow the links.

Antigua

The municipality of Antigua includes the towns of Agua de Bueyes, Las Pocetas, Caleta de Fuste, Las Salinas de El Carmen ,Pozo Negro , Valles de Ortiga, Triquiviaje and Casillas de Morales.

Ayuntamiento

Address

C/ Plaza, nº 1

35630 Antigua

Telephone 928 878233.

Fax 928 878211.

Betancuria

Betancuria includes not only Betancuria, but also Vega de Rio Palmas and Santa Ines.

Ayuntamiento

Address

C/ Amador Rodríguez, nº 4

35637 Betancuria

Telephone 928 878092

Fax 928 878233

La Oliva

The northernmost municipality is La Oliva. This covers the towns of Corralejo, El Cotillo, , Tindaya, La Caldereta, La Jares, El Roque, Vallebron, and Villaverde.

Ayuntamiento

Address

C/ Emilio Castellot Martínez, nº 2

35640 La Oliva.

Telephone 928 681904/905/906.

Fax 928 868035.

Pajara

Pajara is the southermost Municipality and Morro Jable, El Cardon, Toto , Chlegua, La Lajita, Matas Blancas , El Puertito and Ajui are all to be found within the municipality.

Ayuntamiento

Address

C/ Plaza de Regla, s/n

35628 Pájara.

Telephone 928 1614 82/83. .

Fax 928 161474.

Puerto del Rosario

Puerto del Rosario is the municipality that contains the capital of the same name (eponymous, even). Tetir, El Mattoral, El Time, Garcia Escamez, Guisguey, La Matilla, La Ampuyenta, La Asomada, Llanos de la Conception, Puerto Lajas and Tefia and Tesjuante are all found within the municipality.

Ayuntamiento

Address

C/ Fernandez Castaneyra, nº 4

35600 Puerto del Rosario

Telephone 928 850110

Fax 928 850277.

Tuineje

Tuineje includes Gran Tarajal, Giniginamar, Taralejo, Las Playitas, Tiscamanita, La Florida, Tarajalejo, La Fuentita , Catalania Garcia, Las Casitas and El Charco.

Ayuntamiento

Address

Plaza de San Miguel, 1

Telephone 928 164 045/353/354

Fax 928 164 186

Tarajalejo, Fuerteventura

Tarajalejo is becoming quite a large town, spreading out from the original fishing village, which nestled in the lee of the hills to its east.

The hotel Tofio was built adjacent to both the old village and the sea, and the main road originally ran along the coast. The position of the main road has now been changed so that it runs to the north of the hotel and fishing village. A newer development is being built to the north of this road and at the moment, a new layout to the junctions is being created.

There is a large beach, mainly pebbles with some black sand. It is over a kilometre long and averages a width of 45 metres. An old photograph shows that there was an attempt to change it, from its original black sand and pebbles, to a golden sandy beach, but nature wasn't in agreement!

The quay and its sheletered water lies beneath the headland to the east of the town. The quay has a bench built along its length, and in the rocks at the side of the quay, you can see a lot of quite large crabs.

Besides the hotel Tofio, there are a couple of small apartment blocks that have views towards the sea. There are several restaurants and bars in the old town, which maintains its Spanish feel, possibly because the newer part of the town is some distance away on the other side of a busy road.

There is a large town square, where the townsfolk gather during Fiestas etc. The town's annual Fiesta, in celebration of the Sacred Heart, is on the 8th May

Villaverde, Fuerteventura.

Villaverde is just north of La Oliva, on the road between La Oliva and Corralejo. The village is in the hills between the extinct volcanoes of Mount Escanfraga on the east side and Mount Arena on the west side.

The village has grown considerably over the past 15 years and is a thriving village which offers locals and visitors a range of places to visit.

In the past the fertile volcanic soil and the natural underground wells made it an ideal area for growing crops, and is the reason why there are two windmills (now restored) on the escarpment on the south side of the village, for dealing with the grain that needed milling. The windmills present a worthwhile photographic opportunity, and there are excellent views of La Oliva and Mount Tindaya from the ridge.

As it is a large village it has a large supermarket and a smaller supermarket; a rural hotel; seven bars and restaurants; a bakers; a farming co-operative; and three museums.

The local goats cheese is a regular winner of prizes as the island´s best cheese.

The Fiesta of San Vincente is held in the days leading up to April 15.

A walk up Pico de la Zarza, Morro Jable, Fuerteventura

The walk takes around 5 hours and there is no shade. Take food, water and sun protection. The first part of the trip could be done in a 4 wheel drive vehicle.

Begin at this roundabout in Morro Jable. You need to travel up the hill turning left at the Hotel Barcelo and continue up to the water treatment plant. You will then see a wide dirt track road ahead of you. On your left you will have a good view of the new golf course at Morro Jable which nestles between the hills. To your right you will be able to see the windmills at Costa Calma and behind you a great view of Morro Jable. There is plenty of time to admire the view as you will be stopping to catch your breath regularly.

The first bit of the walk is quite steep, after about an hour the terrain is quite different, having almost earth underfoot and there are lots of green plants and gold coloured lichens on the rocks

Towards the end of the walk, after about 3 hours the path becomes quite narrow and steeper. You will come to a gate which you have to unfasten and tie up again. We think this is to keep out the goats which would eat the abundant plants and shrubs that grow particularly well here. There are quite a few small lizards around too.

Once at the top, and you have recovered, you will be treated to fabulous views to the beaches round Cofete and, if you lean a little further over by clinging to the large boulders, you have views of the Villa Winter. After a rest and a bite to eat the walk back is quite quick as it is almost all downhill.

Tamaragua, Fuerteventura

Tamaragua is a large housing development about 5 minutes drive from Corralejo, on the road to Villaverde.

The houses have been built using the volcanic stone as a facing. Each property has its own private garden area, and there are communal garden areas all around Tamaragua. If you are interested in Tamaragua you may wish to ask questions or provide information in the Sunnyfuerteventura forum, Tamaragua thread.

Tamaragua for children

There are children's play areas with the usual array of childrens playground equipment.

Shopping

As you enter the complex there is a large supermarket to your left which carries a wide range of goods.

There is a bar near the entrance to the development and along the road there are a number of retail units which aren´t occupied yet.

Cinema

Behind the supermarket there is a cinema, showing a range of films in Spanish. It is the only cinema in the north of the island.. On Wednesdays you can view the films at discounted prices.

La Pared, Fuerteventura

La Pared is a village on the west coast of Fuerteventura, that has undergone a series of developments which means that it is now relatively large.

The entrance to the village is interesting because when you turn off the main road it is a dirt track for about 200 metres before you reach the tarmacked section. There are a couple of places to eat and a hotel as well as a driving range, where golfers can practise

The west coast of Fuerteventura is subject to larger seas than the east coast and this makes the village an attractive place to those in search of large waves for surfing etc. On the other hand casual bathers need to take a little more care.

There are a couple of beaches, the Playa de Parad and the Playa de Viejo Rey (beach of the old king), and the headland, Punta de Guadalupe, that gives some shelter to the Playa de la Pared, has very interesting geological features.

There is a pretty church named San Benedicto de Ahbed and a childrens play area.

Just north of the town, at Las Hermosas, there is a football stadium where the former Playas de Jandia used to play their home games, before they moved to a stadium in Costa Calma.

Las Playitas, Fuerteventura

When we vistied Las Playitas, it was a small Spanish fishing village with a few houses, typical Spanish bars and restaurants and a majestic lighthouse, El Faro de Entalada, accessible via a lethal trip up a very winding narrow mountain pass, which this intrepid reporter refused to drive back down again.

Just over a year later and the village is still intact, the rest of the bay, which is divided from the village by a headland, however has been taken over as part of the new Bahia Grande luxury facilities. Another large hotel is has now been completed

The hotel has an olympic sized swimming pool, a waterslide and facilities for children.

Las Playitas has a beautiful beach, however the sand is almost black. There are facilites for sailing and diving on the beach.

You can get a bus from Las Playitas to Gran Tarajal.

Tindaya Fuerteventura

Tindaya is a typical Fuerteventuran village, spread over a wide area, in the north of Fuerteventura, set under the sacred Mount Tindaya. The mountain has been declared of Cultural Interest as it was used in the religious practices of the earliest inhabitants of Fuerteventura. Recently, the world-famous sculptor Eduardo Chillida planned to hollow out a 45m x 50m x 65m 'carved space' inside Mount Tindaya to create a unique sculpture, dedicated to tolerance, inside the mountain. The space would not have been visible from the outside, and despite objections it seems that the project will go ahead at some time in the future.

If you want to walk up the mountain you have to make a request to the Ayuntamiento of La Oliva, who will arrange a guide. Besides being a protected area the climb is quite difficult.

Tindaya Village

Tindaya would be an excellent place to take a three year old to teach them about animals. The are a few small holdings, and you can see and or hear, goats, dogs, sheep, chickens, horses, donkeys, lizards, pigeons, cats, and various birds.

Tindaya has three bars, including one called the Tindaya Arms. There is also a small supermarket and a large multi sport facility, as well as a children's play area, which each village seems to have.

The small chapel, Ermita Nuestra Senora de la Caridad, is located at the centre of the village, next to the village square, which is the centre of attention during the villages festivities which are held in August, with the principle day being August 15th.

A car boot sale is held in the village on the 1st Sunday of every month.

The area around Tindaya

Tindaya lies close to the west coast of Fuerteventura, and we are told there is a small beach in the area that is very difficult to find although it is signposted! The area between Tindaya and the coast is important for its birdlife and so you should keep to the track to avoid causing too much disturbance. Most of the coastline in the area is sheer cliff face, which shows some interesting geological features, such as a thin layer of much lighter coloured rock.

The Villa Winter

In the southern part of the island, in Cofete, you can find the legendary Villa Winter. Cofete is a lonely place and the Villa is a mysterious witness of the past. Although the Villa Winter is mentioned in all travelguides, it is not easy to reach. You can only reach it through a bumpy dustroad and with a four-wheel-drive. The place is impressive and massive, two stories high, with notably round arches and a round tower that faces northeast. Architectural details like a coatof arms of the Winter family above the main entrance and a crocodile head cut out of wood make the Villa look like a castle.

Everything started back in the thirties, as German engineer Gustav Winter settled down in Morro Jable, at that time only a little fishing village. Just a few weeks before, he had signed a contract on the Spanish mainland to lease the whole peninsula of Jandia. Gustav Winter was a very conspicuous person who wore dark sunglasses and was always accompanied by a large black dog.

Gustav Winter contributed to the development of Morro Jable and Jandia by building a school and a church and by starting to build a road to end the isolation of the peninsula. He also took the initiative of giving Morro Jable her first proper harbour and planted more than ten thousand pinetrees on the Pico del Zarza, of which none of them are left. Don Gustavo, as he was called by the local inhabitants, recruited men from the nearby villages to built his Villa. It was built under strict secrecy rules. Every morning the builders were brought to the building site and in the evening everyone had to leave the area, with the borders watched by guardesman.

The friendship between Hitler and Franco made it possible, for a major part of the peninsula Jandia to be declared a military zone where no people were allowed. The former inhabitants were driven away without any financial compensation or were forced to move to another village. There is written proof that in 1938 there was a meeting between Winter and the III-Canaris defence. It was agreed that Winter would carry out important economical projects for the third Reich in Jandia and that he was allowed to recruit German workers for that purpose.

For the construction of a road to Cofete political prisoners from the concentration camp in Tefia were used. The mysterious cemetery near the beach has more than once ledto speculation about the working conditions of these men. In 1941 Jandia was bought by "Dehesa de Jandia S.A." who assigned Gustav Winter to be the manager. Both on the premises of the villa and 200 meter to the east, parts of a railway track can be found. So apparently there was also construction work going on on the mountainside.

There is evidence that Fuerteventura, because of the fact that it is favourably situated, should have been a submarine base for the German Navy during the Second World War. It is certain, that there would have been submarines in the waters around the Canary Islands. There is written proof that between March and July 1941 German submarines had been in the harbour of Las Palmas at least six times. It is likely, that the tower of the Villa Winter served as a beacon for submarines and airplanes, that wanted to land on the nearby, little airport of Jandia.

When reading about the history of the Villa Winter, one comes, more than once, across speculations about a possible subterranean submarine harbour. And everyone who knows the geological history of the Canaries, with the many lavatunnels it has got, knows that that might be possible. It is even said, that there are still two complete submarines in it, that officially are claimed to have sunk.

In the seventies, a team consisting of people from Spain and Austria tried to discover the submarines, and lost their lives doing that. It is said that their yacht exploded, but that story was never confirmed. A further indication of a possible military purpose of the villa is the huge fuse box in the upper story of the tower. This fuse box raises the suspicion, that there was equipment in the tower that needed a lot of electricity.

Another persistent rumour tells about the possibility, that the Villa Winter was used as a clinic, where Nazi criminals underwent plastic surgery to change their appearance so they could start a new life in South America. Eyewitnesses claimed to have seen that these ´guests´ were brought up to the coast of Jandia in submarines. But they also might have arrived by plane, because during the last phase of the war, several planes were landing and taking off every night.

Since the nineties the villa has been owned by a Spanish building company. Since that time a warden has lived in the villa, and tourists have been able to a look inside when they pay a small tip. In future the villa will probably be transformed into a hotel or restaurant. Andreas Winter, a distant relative of Gustav Winter, made the attempt to turn the villa into a wellness centre but the Spanish bureaucracy stopped his plans. But no matter how the villa will be used in the future, the myths and legends will always accompany her.

Parque Holandes, Fuerteventura

Parque Holandes lies at the east coast of Fuerteventura between Corralejo and Puerto del Rosario and is part of the municipality of La Oliva. It was designed by a Dutch architect and that's the reason why it is called ´Dutch Park´. Parque Holandes consists of both luxury villas and more basic apartments which can provide affordable rental accommodation as Parque Holandes is located some distance from main tourist resorts. However, you can meet people from all nationalities and all walks of life there.

Getting to Parque Hollandes

Bus number 6 leaves twice an hour from Puerto del Rosario and will take you to Parque Holandes in about 15 minutes. If you only want to spend part of the day here you can get on the same bus again and you will be in Corralejo in another 15 minutes

What you will find in Parque Holandes

As you enter Parque Holandes, you will see an attractive windmill, with a restaurant close by. The wellness center Centro Mirak is next to that. Continuing along the road will bring you past several houses and tourist complexes and on to the shopping centre which forms the heart of Parque Holandes. There are bars, restaurants and a supermarket. In the daytime it is very quiet but in the afternoon and evening the place comes alive and tourists and locals meet at the shopping centre. The other half of Parque Holandes lies further up the hill and you can get some beautiful sea views on the higher ground.

Plans for the area

In the near future, the coastal area near Parque Holandes, of 'El Jablito' might change drastically. Investors from the Spanish mainland are planning to build a private clinic, harbour with sailing school, golf course, beach club and a big hotel. The project is called "La Oliva Sun City Centro de Salud Fuerteventura". If this project is realized it will provide jobs for a lot of people and will give an economic boost to La Oliva. However, there are objections to the plan and this may never take place.

The Centro Cultural de Parque Holandes

The Centro Cultural de Parque Holandes provides a centre for the community. There are Spanish and English lessons, sports and dances arranged, and if you are new to the area then this would be a good place to contact to make new friends and find out what is happening in the area. You will find it at the back of the shopping centre.

Tetir, Fuerteventura

Tetir is a very nice Spanish village that has a mixture of old and new features and is well worth a visit. It is situated 9.2 km, half way along the main road that runs to the west of Puerto del Rosario.

The church was built at the beginning of the 18th century under the patronage of Santo Domingo de Guzmán, and takes its name from him. It has a single nave with a tiled roof. The presbitary is higher than the nave, with a four sloped roof. The front facade is the bell tower that was built in 1880 is formed from various layers one on top of the other which get smaller as the tower goes up. It is quite pretty inside.

Four times a year there is a Mercado Artesanal or craft fayre. Here you can buy typical canarian products and other goods that are made on the island. While you are there you can have a camel ride or a ride on a donkey cart and listen to some Canarian folk music. The market is held on the second SUnday of March, June, September and December.

Tetir is in the municipality of Puerto del Rosario, about 10km from the capital itself.

There are several bars, a supermarket and a nice Spanish bakery where we had a nice cake! It has the normal childrens' play area and a large hall for lucha canaria, - Canarian wrestling.

Triquivijate, Fuerteventura

Triquivijate, known to the British as Tricky, because it is difficult to pronounce and spell, is 11 km from Caleta off the road to Antigua.

It has grown from what used to be a farming village into a more diverse community. You can see evidenco of its farming origins from the cactus plantation near the roundabout and of the roundabout itself which is based on pitchforks.

It is similar to Lajares in that it is a widespread village which is popular with a lot of expats from different countries. There are a few luxury properties, some traditional ones and some smaller properties.

There are several bars and restaurants along the main road through the village, a shop, ferreteria etc.

There is a cultural centre, with hopscotch in case you are nostalgic for your childhood (or maybe its for the children) which offers a range of activities, and next to it is the chapel.

There is a horse riding and excursion centre with a paddock with horses and as you drive out of the village there is pond which is a good birdwatching site. Sadly the pond was empty of water when we went, but the reeds were quite visible. After heavy rain it does fill up.

Puerto Lajas, Fuerteventura

Puerto Lajas is quite a large town just to the north of Puerto del Rosario. It is stretched out into a couple of streets lining the rocky shore.

It is inhabited mainy by Spanish people and last Sunday, 12th October they held their annual festival. This festival is when the statue of Ntra Sra del Pino is taken from the church onto a boat and taken around the harbour to bless it and to ensure the safety of those using the harbour and good catches for the fishermen.

In Puerto Lajas that day there was a very large crowd of people many of them wearing traditional Canarian dress. There was also a market of Traditional Canarian goods.

Puerto Lajares itself seems to have grown quite a bit recently, from its origins as a fishing village, and many of the houses there are quite new. It also has a small church.

Betancuria, Fuerteventura

Betancuria, founded in 1405 by the Norman Conqueror Jean de Bethancourt, was once the capital of the island of Fuerteventura. Now it governs the municipality of Betancuria, which includes the towns

Vega de Rio Palmas and Valle de Santa Ines, as well as Betancuria itself.

The region is renowned for its mountains and stunning views, and is a sparsely populated region with only a few hundred inhabitants. Montana de la Atalaya is its highest mountain standing at 724 metres.

Betancuria contains several important religious buildings including the Iglesia de Santa Maria de Betancuria and the convent of San Buenaventura, which originated in 1416.It was consecrated as a cathedral in 1426. Pope Martin the fifth appointed it a BIshops seat, but the positon was never taken up.

Betancuria is well worth a visit. It appeals to the sort of tourist that like to go looking at churches and museums, and there are several bars and cafes that cater for the needs of tourists. The setting is idyllic, or as close as you can get to it on such a dry island.

On the drive out of Betancuria as you head north up the mountainside, there is an excellent viewpoint which overlooks Betancuria to the south and the Tefia plain to the north. There are two giant statues here of Ayoze and Guisgey who used to rule the two kingdoms of Fuerteventura.

Around the next bend there is a turning to the right. This is a road up to the Mirador Morro Velosa which is a building designed by Caesar Manrique the famed architect from Lanzarote, which sits on top Mount Tegu 500 metres above sea level. It is a lookout point, a cafe and an exhibition centre that sits right on top of the mountain. There are wonderful views to the east towards Caleta de Fuste, and to the north over the Tefia plain towards Tindaya Mountain in the north.

Fiestas

Place	Fiesta of	Date
Betancuria	San Buenaventura	14th July
Betancuria	Nuestra Senora de la Immaculada Concepcion	8th December
Valle de Santa Ines	Santa Ines	21st January
Valle de Santa Ines	San Bartolome	24th August
Vaga de Rio Palmas	San Sebastian	20th January
Vaga de Rio Palmas	Virgin de La Pina	5th August
Vaga de Rio Palmas	San Lorenzo	10th August

Vaga de Rio Palmas	La Pina procession.(Island Fiesta)	3rd Saturday in September
Vaga de Rio Palmas	Santa Lucia	13th September
Vaga de Rio Palmas	Appearance of the Virgin Mary	18th December

Pozo Negro, Fuerteventura

Pozo Negro is a small village inhabited mostly by locals. It is about half an hours drive towards Morro Jable from Caleta, turn left when you get to the experimental granga, wich is the place where they research various foodstuffs. Somemthing they are working on currently is the positive effects camel milk can have on sugar levels in those with diabetes.

When we were there there was a large catamaran moored just away from the small beach, where a few of the locals were sunbathing. Much of the rest of the beach ar eawas covered in pebbles. Many of them were also enjoying the local restaurant as it was Sunday. The village also has a children's play area.

Ajuy, Fuerteventura

Ajuy is a small village on the West coast of Fuerteventura. It is less than a twenty minute drive from Pajara, most of the drive is along the valley which has Ajuy at its mouth.

The beach at Ajuy is attractive, though covered with black sand. A couple of the few restaurants in the village are on or close to the beach.

The village is probably most visited because of the caves that are to be found a short walk from the town. The path to the caves is to be found at the northern end of the beach, and leads past the hut that has been built into the rock face.

The views from the path are quite impressive, as the coast in this area consists mainly of cliffs.

The caves are quite impressive, and can be entered via a series of steps that have to be navigated with care. We are not sure that it is sensible to enter the caves without some sort of protective head gear that a speliologist would wear as a matter of course.

Beaches
La Concha beach on the Isle of Lobos
Bathe on a sandy beach on the Isle of Lobos

The main beach on the Isle of Lobos, north of Fuerteventura, is an ideal place to start the day, then continue to explore this uninhabited island of 4.5 square kilometres. It's also a good idea to end your excursion around this scarcely populated islet, only accessible by boat, with a refreshing dip. Either way it's very advisable to take the opportunity to enjoy the generally calm - and at times - totally still Atlantic and this legendary beach of virtually white sand, offering over a kilometre of tranquillity.

The best beach on Lobos with views of Fuerteventura
The beach of La Concha is situated just a 10-minute walk from the ferry that links to Corralejo and just over 15 minutes' walk to the island's small harbour. Its semi-circular shape provides a level of protection that is the key to the transparency of its waters with its many shades of blue. On this noticeably deserted island of almost permanent sunshine, the chance to cool off in this oasis, whether you're alone or in company, will bring you back to life. Some people even choose to camp here, and many are quick to return to this delightful spot.

Viejo Rey beach
A fabulous surf beach in south-east Fuerteventura

While windsurfing and kitesurfing monopolise the beaches of Corralejo and the south of Jandia, the Viejo Rey beach has always been the legendary surfing capital of Fuerteventura. Located in La Pared, an enclave named after the wall that dissected the island in two in times gone by, this beach of almost a kilometre in length is not only a benchmark for surfers, but also for lovers of freedom and nudism, as there is plenty of space for everybody.

Bathe in one of Jandía's nudist beaches

The strong winds and frequent waves justify the beach's status as a surfing destination, but also means that care should be taken while swimming here. Jandía's black, and in certain areas, golden sands, its vast open expanses, guaranteed sun and refreshing ocean are the perfect combination to encourage visitors to unwind, take a stroll and enjoy the day. Viejo Rey beach is located near the residential area of La Pared and there is also another bay nearby, which adds to area's charm.

Corralejo's Big Beaches (Grandes Playas de Corralejo)

Large, heavenly beaches in the north of Fuerteventura

Very close to the tourist hub of Corralejo, in the north-east of Fuerteventura, you can enjoy the internationally known 'Grandes

Playas' - Big Beaches of Corralejo; nine kilometres of divine beaches bordered by the Corralejo Dunes, the largest in the Canary Islands. This is a place where the turquoise waters lap a coast covered by fine white sand formed naturally from the erosion of sea shells. Excellent for exfoliation, this particular form of sand has made these beaches an authentic natural spa, with views of the islands of Los Lobos and Lanzarote.

Family beaches and sporting beaches close to Corralejo
Corralejo's Big Beaches are formed by a number of beaches in the Corralejo Natural Park, accessible from the FV-1 motorway, with parking alongside. The small coves towards the south end are perfect for nudist bathing in complete privacy. Travel northwards and the beaches are more family-friendly and have services such as lifeguards, in Burro beach for example, or a more complete range including sunbed and parasol hire in the Bajo Negro beach in front of the Riu hotels. El Médano beach, the closest to Corralejo, is mainly used by those who practise water sports such as kite boarding and windsurf.

La Guirra

A perfect beach for the little ones
The beach at La Guirra is located right next to Caleta de Fuste, meaning that it is very close to all of the amenities that this popular

resort offers. Positioned on the east coast of Fuerteventura, it is one of the island's most popular beaches for small children as the sea is so calm that they can safely play and splash around all day. Seven hundred metres of soft white sand make this beach the perfect place for a day spent having fun in the sun.

Amphibious chair service in Fuerteventura
The beach provides sun loungers with parasols anchored in the sand and a parking area. It also has lifeguards and amphibious chairs, allowing people with reduced mobility to enjoy the sea to the full. A landscaped promenade, decorated with old lime kilns surrounds the area around La Guirra beach and connects with the centre of Caleta de Fuste, where visitors will find a wide range of leisure options and restaurants.

Cofete beach
A wild twelve-kilometre beach in Fuerteventura
As one of the wildest beaches in the Canaries, with the largest dimensions and least urban developments, it is hard to find the adjectives to Cofete beach justice. Located in the north of the Jandia peninsula in the south of Fuerteventura, Cofete is a visual feast of endless golden sand, wild seas and a wonderful sense of freedom. Its twelve kilometres, the scarcity of houses, lack of paved roads and the

need for a 4x4 to get there says everything about it. The term 'virgin' was invented for this beach.

Swim next to the mountains of Jandía

Reaching Cofete is not easy: the road is made up of dirt and rocks. It runs for 8.5 kilometres, with difficult sections, but it is surmountable if skilled. Those who dare to venture it will be rewarded with awed amazement as they take in the immensity of the mountains of Jandia, the cape known as El Islote and the fury of the Atlantic, which should be treated with the utmost respect. After passing through a small village with a restaurant, all that is left to do is park the car and enjoy long walks north or south. A stunning beach that more than justifies the effort to get there.

Esquinzo Butihondo beach

A semi-urban beach where nude bathing is common

Esquinzo Butihondo beach is close to the Esquinzo Butihondo development, to the north of the large tourist town of Morro Jable. It's a semi-urban beach spanning almost three kilometres, divided into different sections, which allow large areas of seclusion and tranquillity even though you are in a tourist zone. For this reason, the beach, situated in the south of the island, is perfect for nudist bathing in complete privacy, for sunbathing or practising a variety of water sports.

Golden sands and calm turquoise waters beside Morro Jable
Esquinzo Butihondo is a golden sand beach with peaceful blue waters. It offers a range of services allowing you spend the whole day on the beach, with sunbed and parasol hire, showers and toilets. There are a number of small bars dotted along the beach where you can eat beside the sea as well as stalls offering water sport equipment hire and classes. There is also an extensive range of hotel and apartment accommodation. The beach is very accessible, with parking facilities and a public bus service linking the beach to Morro Jable.

La Guirra

A perfect beach for the little ones
The beach at La Guirra is located right next to Caleta de Fuste, meaning that it is very close to all of the amenities that this popular resort offers. Positioned on the east coast of Fuerteventura, it is one of the island's most popular beaches for small children as the sea is so calm that they can safely play and splash around all day. Seven hundred metres of soft white sand make this beach the perfect place for a day spent having fun in the sun.

Amphibious chair service in Fuerteventura

The beach provides sun loungers with parasols anchored in the sand and a parking area. It also has lifeguards and amphibious chairs, allowing people with reduced mobility to enjoy the sea to the full. A landscaped promenade, decorated with old lime kilns surrounds the area around La Guirra beach and connects with the centre of Caleta de Fuste, where visitors will find a wide range of leisure options and restaurants.

Morro Jable beach

An exotic beach near excellent shopping facilities in Fuerteventura
In the large tourist area of Morro Jable, in the south of Fuerteventura, you will find a huge white sand beach with tranquil waters, shimmering shades of turquoise and emerald. This is Morro Jable beach and it stretches from Las Gaviotas beach in the north to the centre of the coastal town of Morro Jable, in the south. Running alongside the kilometres-long beach is an avenue with excellent shopping facilities and a view of the emblematic Morro Jable lighthouse, standing out from the sea.

Four kilometres of tourist beach beside the Jandía salt marsh
The Morro Jable beach extends for four kilometres and is bordered by an enormous avenue with shops, leisure areas and restaurants, and the Jandía salt marsh, an 'Area of Scientific Interest' for the

conservation of a scarce plant in the Canary Islands that is resistant to salt water. A tourist beach with lifeguards, sunbeds and parasols for hire, small beach bars and several areas for water sports such as surfing or canoeing. The best way to enjoy this beach? Stay in a hotel nearby to spend a blissful day out at the beach, and then finish off with a quiet dinner beside the sea as the sun sets.

Sotavento beach

Nine kilometres of Virgin beach in Fuerteventura
Fuerteventura could be described in a single word: beaches. Describing the incredible vista of Sotavento is easy: it's the islands best known beach in the world. Just its length, about nine kilometres, leaves visitors speechless. At low tide, the island gains so much land that some residents doubt that Tenerife is the largest of the Canary Islands. The huge lagoons that are created at low tide, the constant sunshine and infinite golden sand make it worthy of another synonym: paradise.

The best windsurfing and kitesurfing beach in Jandía
In reality, Sotavento is made up of five beaches: La Barca, Risco del Paso, Mirador, Los Canarios and Malnombre. With endless walks next to its clear waters there is no need to wait for low tide. A sand barrier at 100 and 300 metres from the shore creates a lagoon three

kilometres long, perfect for beginners to windsurfing or kitesurfing; of which there are many. Turn around and take in a wonderful scene of solitude, with thousands of metres of sand and ocean before you. A real treat.

La Concha beach, El Cotillo

One of Fuerteventura's best-known beaches
In the north-east of Fuerteventura you will find the beaches of the coastal village of El Cotillo. To the north they extend into a series of family-friendly coves of white sand and calm turquoise waters. La Concha beach is one of them, and is one of the best-known in Fuerteventura for its beauty, quality and tranquillity. The beach's close proximity to the town allows you enjoy a break with incredible sea views and amazing sunsets, where the sky changes from ochre to violet in a matter of minutes.

A white sand cove for all the family in El Cotillo
La Concha beach enjoys gentle waves thanks to its natural horseshoe-shaped reef. When the wind picks up the 'corralitos', small circular walls made from volcanic rock built by residents, are the perfect refuge, and at low tide the smallest members of the family can play safely in the small rock pools that form. There is parking very close to

the beach and a lifeguard service as well as apartments and a restaurant nearby.

Corralejo Viejo

An easily accessible, tranquil beach in Fuerteventura
Spend a day at Corralejo Viejo, a beach in the north of Fuerteventura where everybody can enjoy the sea and sun. This pleasant beach is known for its accessibility and safety: the turquoise waters are so calm that a swim here is like bathing in a still pool. The tranquillity found in this cove guarantees relaxation while the children run through the sand and make the most of their holiday in Fuerteventura.

Shopping and easy parking next to the beach
The beach area located in the tourist resort of Corralejo has walkways and ramps to facilitate access onto the sand for those with pushchairs or wheelchairs. There's a team of people dedicated to helping people with disabilities enabling them to enjoy a relaxing day on the beach in Corralejo Viejo. Toilets, showers and parking is provided, and the beach is positioned alongside an avenue where there are plenty of cafés and shops

Costa Calma beach

Two kilometres of tourist beach close to La Lajita

Situated in the south of Furteventura, close to the town of La Lajita, you'll find Playa de Costa Calma Costa Calma beach - two kilometres of white sand and refreshing turquoise waters. Its idyllic shoreline invites you to stroll along the sand, admiring the impressive views of a coastline full of ochre mountains, smoothed by years of erosion. Protected from the wind by the hotels and apartments, a dip in the sea is just a few short sandy steps away from your hotel terrace or pool.

A sandy white beach with water sports in Fuerteventura
Costa Calma beach is just one of a number of stretches that are linked during low tide. In the northern section there are two small family beaches. When the wind picks up, the southern section is perfect for surfing and windsurfing lessons. The range of accommodation available near the beach ensures an excellent range of services such as sunbeds and parasols for hire, lifeguard cover, and lots of water-based activities. The access road is flanked by local vegetation making Costa Calma an authentic oasis in the white sand.

Weather in Fuerteventura

Fuerteventura enjoys year-round good weather, with temperatures in the winter months on a par with those in the UK in the summer months. With very little rain and plenty of sunshine, it is a great option for those looking for guaranteed (well nearly!) blue skies and warm weather.

Being so close to the Sahara, it can experience sandstorms but these tend to occur relatively infrequently and do not last long. This location can also lead to dust storms, particularly in the Spring, which last on average two to four days, although do occasionally last longer. The main potential issue is visibility, which can affect flights. However, the island's proximity to the Sahara does mean it has some fantastic sandy beaches.

Temperatures

The average temperature for May to October is 23.5°C, with August and September being the hottest months with an average temperature of 25°C. Winter months tend to see a slightly cooler average temperature of 19°C but this is still the average temperature for July and August in London!

Sunshine

With an annual average of nearly 8 hours of sunshine, Fuerteventura enjoys plenty more of sunshine than the UK, especially during the winter. The graph below compares the numbers of hours sunshine per day in Fuerteventura compared to London.

Rainfall

Fuerteventura is very lucky in that it has very little rain and often no rain at all during the summer, so rain is unlikely to be a problem on your holiday. The graph sets out the average number of rain days per month.

Accommodation: Hotel and Beach Resort

Barceló Castillo Beach Resort

The Barceló Castillo Beach Resort hotel is situated on the Caleta de Fuste beachfront and is an ideal hotel for families to enjoy the excellent local watersports. There is a good choice of rooms, including a two-bedroom bungalow, which allows you to enjoy time together in the evening once the children are in bed.

The hotel is next door to the "El Castillo" Marina where you will find a wide range of activities, such as boat trips, fishing and diving. There is also a good selection of onsite activities, including three swimming pools and separate children's pools, mini golf, beach volley ball and snorkelling.

There is Kids Club run by the hotel for children aged 4 to 12, which is open for two hours per morning and afternoon. There is also a babysitting service available and daytime and evening entertainment

Time for You

Make use of the hotel's Kids Club or leave your little ones with your other half and enjoy a couple of hours relaxing in the onsite Thalasso Spa.

In a Nutshell

- Two bedroom bungalows available
- Beachfront location
- Close to airport
- World-class diving location
- Hotel run Kids Club (ages 4 - 12)
- Three swimming pools
- Separate children's pools
- Babysitting available
- All-inclusive option
- Thalasso Spa

ClubHotel Riu Oliva Beach Resort

The ClubHotel Riu Oliva Beach Resort is situated on the beautiful Playa de Corralejo beach, on the island of Fuerteventura. This family-friendly hotel enjoys a quiet location away from the main resort but has plenty of on-site entertainment for all the family.

There are family rooms with separate bedrooms, sleeping up to 5 people, as well as suites with a separate lounge area. So, it is ideal for parents looking for a little privacy in the evenings.

The hotel's entertainment programme provides a wide range of both daytime and evening activities for all ages. There are plenty of sporting options, including Riu Fit fitness classes, beach volleyball and a multi-sports court. For those of you who are less sporty, there is the Riu Art art workshops that are held several times a week.

The hotel runs its own kids' clubs, called the Riu Land programme. Here children from ages 4 to 12 are kept entertained with various fun activities. There is also an evening entertainment programme with live shows, as well as a mini-disco for the children and a late-night disco for the older guests.

The ClubHotel Riu Oliva Beach Hotel's location on Playa de Corralejo beach makes it an ideal spot for trying out some water sports, including windsurfing, diving, surfing and kite surfing. And with two main pools, plus two children's pools, all of which are heated in winter, there's plenty of opportunity for swimming and splashing about in the water.

The ClubHotel Riu Oliva Beach Resort is a great option for those families who prefer to be based outside of the resort centre.

However, the popular town of Corralejo is within easy reach by a bus that stops right outside the hotel.

Time for You

Pop the children into bed in their own room and enjoy an evening watching the sun go down over a chilled glass of wine.

In a Nutshell

- Rooms with 1 or 2 bedrooms available
- Situated on Grandes Playas sand dune beach
- Two swimming pools (450 m2 and 400 m2)
- Two children's swimming pools
- Pools heated in winter
- Art workshops
- Daytime activity programme
- Awarded GOLD certification for the Travelife Sustainability System
- RiuLand Kids' Club (ages 4 to 7 & 8 to 12)
- Surrounded by a 35,000 m2 garden

Iberostar Fuerteventura Palace

The Iberostar Fuerteventura Palace is located in Jandia, in the south of the island of Fuerteventura. Situated on the beachfront on Playa de Jandia, a white sand beach over 15 miles long, this family-friendly hotel enjoys gorgeous seaviews and boasts a relaxing and luxurious atmosphere.

There are three pools to choose from, plus a separate children's pool, which is heated in winter. There is an onsite scuba diving school meaning you don't have to wander far to enjoy some fantastic water sports.

There are hotel runs kids clubs for children from ages 4 to 17 and the hotel also offers babysitting services in the evening for children aged 2 to 12.

If you are holidaying with older children (over the age of 16) then you can treat yourself to staying in the Star Prestige area, with exclusive benefits including premium amenities in the room, exclusive pool and sunbathing area with private access, free Wi-Fi and free late check-out.

Time for You

Let the children burn off some energy in the Kids Clubs while you enjoy learning to scuba dive or, if you are feeling less energetic, relaxing in the hotel spa.

In a Nutshell

- Interconnecting family rooms available
- Beachfront location
- 3 swimming pools
- Separate children's pool
- All-inclusive option
- Onsite scuba diving school
- Spa Sensations Thai Zen
- Kids Clubs (4 to 17)
- Evening childcare facilities available (2 to 12)
- Golf courses nearby

Hotel Riu Palace Tres Islas

Located in the beautiful sand dunes of the Playa de Corralejo, the Hotel Riu Palace Tres Islas offers fantastic views of the sea. An ideal location for a family beach holiday and one that has inspired many photographers and TV advertisements.

The hotel has suites with separate bedrooms, which is great for families looking for more space and privacy in their family hotel room.

A primary aim of the Hotel Riu Palace Tres Islas is to provide a place for you to relax and enjoy a well-earned rest. During the month of August there is a Kids Club for children aged 4 to 12. There's also an adults-only spa, the Renova Spa, offering a range of treatments and facilities for those looking for some "me-time".

For those looking for more energetic activities, there's table tennis and a gym. There is also the opportunity to learn tennis at the onsite tennis school or you can partake in various watersports in the local area, such as windsurfing or diving, or enjoy the scenery while you play some golf.

There are also two pools with fantastic views of the sea, as well as separate children's pool. The children's pool and one of the main pools are heated in winter, meaning you can still enjoy a swim even if the outside temperature is a little cooler great for younger children in particular.

You can stay on a bed & breakfast or half board option, with the latter allowing you to enjoy the buffet-style restaurant. There are themed evenings, as well as the "Krystal" fusion restaurant.

Overall, this is hotel designed more for families looking for some relaxation and quiet time than those looking for full-on activities.

However, there are lots of activities on offer in the local area for those who are looking for something more energetic.

Time for You

If you are travelling in August with school age children, let them run off some energy in the Kids Club while you recharge your batteries at the onsite Renova Spa.

In a Nutshell

- Rooms with separate bedroom available
- Situated on Grandes Playas sand dune beach
- Renova Spa (adults only)
- Sea view pools
- Pools heated in winter
- Kids Club (ages 4-12, six times a week in August)
- Tennis School
- Free Wi-Fi
- Live evening entertainment
- Completely renovated in 2008

Iberostar Playa Gaviotas

The IBEROSTAR Playa Gaviotas hotel enjoys a beach front location, being situated right on the beach of Playa de Jandia. This all-inclusive hotel is designed for both families and couples, with a wide range of activities on offer for all ages.

There are Kids Clubs for children starting from age 4 and up to age 17 and for adults there is a wonderful spa and plenty of entertainment. There's even a bowling alley where you enjoy some family time.

There is a choice of rooms, including interconnecting family rooms, allowing you to all have your own space. There is also the new Star Prestige area for families with children over 14, offering refurbished rooms and exclusive services.

Time for You
With such a wide choice of activities, let the children have fun in the Kids Clubs and try something new.

In a Nutshell
- Rooms with a separate sleeping area available
- All inclusive
- Children's Pool
- Children's Clubs (from ages 4 to 17)
- Mini-disco

- Live music
- Weekly casino nights
- Bowling, snooker & table football
- Spa Sensations Thai Zen
- Supermarket, post office & doctor onsite

H10 Tindaya

An ideal family hotel for those looking for a more peaceful location, the H10 Tindaya hotel is located on Fuerteventura's turquoise coast, Costa Calma.

There are family rooms available that have a separate bedroom and benefit from a modern interior design.

The Daisy Miniclub is open to children aged 4 to 7 years and offers a range of activities to entertain younger guests, including a playground, board games, painting and crafts. There are also two children's pools and a minidisco.

For older guests, the Despacio Thalasso spa offers a wide range of treatments and has a thermal area with sauna and Turkish bath. There is a charge for entry unless you opt for the All Inclusive Service Plus, in which case guests are allowed daily access to the spa free of charge.

The spa is open to over-16s only except for the daily family session from 10.30am to 1.30pm.

There is direct access to a beautiful sandy beach (although look out for nudists!) and the small town of Costa Calma is in walking distance. As the name suggests, it is a relatively calm area of the island (apart from the wind) so ideal for those looking for a more relaxing holiday or a great base to explore the rest of the island if you opt to hire a car.

Time for You

Let the children burn off some energy at the minidisco before bed while you enjoy an evening glass of wine.

In a Nutshell

- Rooms with separate sleeping areas
- 3 outdoor pools (one heated in winter)
- 2 children's pools
- All inclusive
- Despacio Thalasso Centre
- Hotel-run Miniclub (Ages 4-12)
- Free wi-fi in lobby & reception area
- Evening entertainment
- Children's playground

➢ Miniclub

Excursions on Fuerteventura and Lanzarote

Why spend hours walking around searching for that special excursion that you so deserve

We reckon that your holiday has been well earned (especially in these tough times), and every minute of it should be spent doing the things that you want to do.

Excursions on both islands

We offers you a great choice of the most interesting excursions on Fuerteventura and Lanzarote, from visiting live volcanos to Dolphin spotting.

Most excursions listed below include transportation, insurance, lunch, and entrance fees and a guide that speaks your language.

Simply click on the excursion(s) you fancy, book your place using the form that can be found on the information page of each excursion. We'll get back to you and confirm the exact date, pick-up time and the nearest pick-up point to your holiday resort and provide secure online payment details.

Remember some trips do sell out or only operate on certain dates.
!!!Our advice is to be prepared, book early and don't miss out! ENJOY!

Volcano Express - Lanzarote

From Corralejo catch the ferry to Playa Blanca, a bus will bring you to the Natural Park of Timanfaya crossing the incredible Lava landscape. You'll get a guided tour across the park to see the different volcanos and craters.

Few demonstrations will be done to show you the immense power of the heat just below the surface.

You will have time to go to a natural oven, where food is cooked, and to have a look around at the magnificent craters with the best views of those striking lava fields !

This visit is very interesting for all the family leaving you feeling you've just been to another world !

After the tour, the bus will take you back to Playa Blanca where you can take the next ferry or enjoy the last one at 19:00 to spend more time in Lanzarote !

Fuerteventura - Sport Fishing*Enjoy the best spots to fish!*
Take all the family on board. All equipment is also provided. Just relax and enjoy !

For a full 5 hours, on an full equipped fishing boat you will be taken to the very best spots to enjoy your favourite sport!

All the family can join in on this fantastic experience!

Different prices for fishers and accompanying persons..!

Don't forget your camera!

Fuertescout *Nature-walks*

Tired of just sitting around by the pool? Then get up and give us a call!

Fuertescout, founded by licensed guide Andreas Caliman, offers:

Guided van tours (up to eight clients) volcanos, virgin beaches and spots of interest off the beaten track.

For professionals, we offer:

Location scouting (photography, television)

Customized trips (journalists, scientists and businessmen)

Andreas Caliman is a government-licensed tour guide for Fuerteventura, giving tours in English, German and Spanish. He has led over 1,000 tours from groups of two to fifty.

Lanzarote Grand Tour - Days of Excursion - Tue / Sat

Discover Lanzarote it's volcano and more..

This great day out takes you to the beautiful bay of El Golfo, where the Olivin stone was found.

Discover the hot springs and salt flats in Janubio where you will learn about the importance of salt extraction and more on the island's history.

Next on the list is the famous Timanfaya National Park, home to Fire Mountain where you will see the geothermal experiments, demonstrating the immense power of the intense heat just below the surface.

There's plenty of time to visit the natural oven, where food is cooked on the heat of the volcano, and do your own bit of exploring before the coach takes you on the magnificent crater tour with the very best views of the lava fields.

A great 3 course lunch is provided in a typical Canarian village before making your way through La Geria, with it's strange vineyards, here you'll discover the history and process of the wine-making with the opportunity to taste the wines and to purchase them.

Passing the monument Al Campesino, in the centre of the island, we head northbound, though Teguise, the ancient capital, arriving at the highest point, Peñas del Chache (670m). From this viewpoint, you will be able to take photos of the north-east coastline and Haria, the valley of 1000 palms. Through the winding roads we make our way to the mirador of Guinate, another spectacular viewpoint. This looks out onto the Chinijo Islands; Alegranza, Montaña Clara and La Graciosa (the latter being the only one inhabited).

Our visit to Los Jameos del Agua is a great end to the day. Here, the gifted Cesar Manrique has left his mark. Enchanting subterranean gardens and the magnificent auditorium are examples of the artist's genius. Los Jameos is also the home to the blind albino crab. Don't forget to look around 'La Casa de los Volcanes', dedicated to volcanology studies.

Departure from Lanzarote is at 6pm and you arrive back on Fuerteventura at about 6.30pm.

Included in the itinerary:

- Ferry fare
- Entrance to the Timanfaya National Park
- Entrance to Los Jameos del Agua
- Wine tasting
- 3 course lunch
- Experienced english-speaking guide
- Modern bus with air conditioning
- Insurance

Zoo - Oasis Park The real natural paradise on earth, more than 70 000 m2 !

There are many many animals here including Hippopotamuses, Giraffes and over 200 different species of birds !

As well as the zoo, the park also has a botanical garden centre, Sea Lions and a variety of other shows.

You will enjoy an unforgettable day visiting one of the most important projects created to protect and preserve the unique flora and fauna of the Canary Islands.

Oasis Park offers you a lot of interesting and very entertaining shows and of course don't forget our camel safari - the highlight of the day!

Oasis Park overview: - Animal Park, African Savannah, Botanical Garden, Sea Lion Show, Parrot Show, Birds of Prey Display, Reptile Show, Camel Safari.

This truly is an unforgettable day in the south of the Island.

Fuerteventura Grand Tour - (Mondays only)

The best way to discover this wonderful island!
On departing CORRALEJO, you will head along the main road towards the south of the island, passing LA OLIVA to stop at the sacred mountain called "TINDAYA".

Next up is a traditional local farm where we you have the chance to savour the famous local goat cheese and see the goats in their natural habitat.

Then it's on to the former capital of BETANCURIA where time seems to stand still! Here you will have time to explore, buy some souvenirs or simply chill out with a drink.

Then after a short drive through Betancuria to reach PAJARA, a real green oasis at the foot of the mountains, you'll visit the tiny Nuestra Señora de la Regla church, with her unique aztek portal.

Right outside the town the next stop is at the Aloe vera factory.

After the lunch (not included), you will follow the road to "La Pared" (the wall) which is a reminder of the ancient border between the north and the south of the Island.

The home route will take you through the centre of the Island and continuing onto the Eastern coast, passing by CALETA DE FUSTE, PUERTO DEL ROSARIO (the new Capital) and finally the beautiful sand dunes of CORRALEJO!

You will be back to where you started your day at around about 16.30hrs.

Included in the itinerary:

- Tour companion
- Cheese Tasting
- Aloe Vera Factory
- Modern bus with air conditioning
- Insurance

Lanzarote Ferry - Playa Blanca - 30 MinGet to Lanzarote in only 30 minutes!

Make the most of our incredible discounted prices, and take the 30 minute ferry ride from Lanzarote's Playa Blanca !

Why not see two islands in one holiday?

Spend the day in Lanzarote, shopping, on the beach, in a bar, restaurant or simply taking in some of the sights Lanzarote has to offer.

Feel free to browse around and return on the ferry to Fuerteventura at 15:00pm, 17:00pm and 19:00pm.

Fuerteventura Airport.

When you have arrived at an airport it is nice to have some idea of what to expect. This page gives a little information about the facilities at Fuerteventura airport.

Fuerteventura airport has recently had a massive extension that more or less doubled its capacity. The new extension has been opened, though work is still going on to reassign parts of the old building to different requirements. It is now large and spacious and has the capacity to cope with the expected growth over the next twenty years.

Flight Arrivals

The first thing you do when you arrive at Fuerteventura Airport is to pass through immigration control. This procedure is smoothly carried out and you once you have passed through the checkpoint you will enter the baggage collection area. You will get information as to which conveyor your luggage will arrive on. This area has lots of toilets, and you can also find information about such things as taxi prices from the airport to various destinations. There is help available should your luggage be lost or damaged in transit.

Travelling onto your resort

Once you have picked up your luggage there are two sets of automatic doors will allow you out of the controlled area. Please note that when you leave this area airport security will not allow you back in so please make sure you have collected all your luggage. If you have a tour operator then they will greet you just outside these doors. The coach car park is just outside the terminal building to the right, and as it is now a big building it's best to make use of the trolleys. These cost €1 andalso take pound coins; you will get your money back when you return it to the trolley park areas.

When you exit the baggage collection area, and if you have flown with a holiday company, the reps will be waiting for you here. If you have hired a car, that is to be picked up from the airport, the car hire offices are between the two exits. To your right are various desks used by different tour companies on different days.

Fuerteventura Airport Taxis

For those making their own way to their resort there is a taxi rank outside the Arrivals.. Although the queues, at peak times, seem quite long, there are plenty of taxis and they come along every few minutes so you will not be waiting long. Taxis are strictly controlled and have meters so you will know how much they cost. For up to date taxi prices see our Transportation page.

Fuerteventura Airport Bus

There are no trains on Fuerteventura so your other option to get to your resort is to use the local bus service which is very reliable and cheap. The bus timetables can be found from our Getting About page. The buses at the airport go to Caleta de Fuste, Puerto del Rosario and Morro Jable (via Costa Calma). You can get other connecting buses in

Puerto del Rosario at the bus station, where all bus routes start and finish.

Fuerteventura Airport Car Hire

The car hire firms that have offices in the airport have windows in the baggage collection area, or you can speak to them outside the baggage area. There are several car hire companies to choose from, it's probably best to book in advance at peak times as sometimes there are no cars available for hire, You can do this via the Sunnyfuerteventura Car Hire facility using the logo on the left. You can pick your car up from the car park, just outside the terminal.

Fuerteventura Airport Car Parking

There is a large car parking area in front of the airport which is covered and has 1,300 parking spaces for private and hired cars.

Parking charges are very reasonable, the first half hour is free; then 0.015319 cents a minute from 31 to 60 minutes; 0.014362 cents a minute from 61 minutes, with a maximum daily price of €8.40 (for up to 4 days). The daily maximum from the fifth day is €6.70. The car park payment is via automatic payment machines or at the payment kisok which has a large blue sign above it.

There are four automatic payment machines. Two are outside, opposite Arrivals; and two are inside, one in the Arrivals and another in the Departures area. The payment machines accept euro bank notes and coins; the kiosk will accept credit cards. After paying you have 20 minutes to leave the car park. You exit the car park by putting your ticket into the machine, which allows the barrier to lift.

Catering

To the right of the airport building you can find a good restaurant tucked away. Inside the terminal building there is a large cafe where you can buy refreshments and there is also a chemist, bookshop, informaion desk and an interesting fish tank! If you or the airport staff have any concerns about your fitness to fly then there is a doctor on hand to examine you.

After you go through the security area you will find a variety of places to eat and lots of shops.

Departure flights

When it is time to get your flight home, the first thing to do is to find your flight on the departures board. There will be a range of gates indicated for your flight. You can queue in any of these, as whichever one you choose will be the slowest, or is that just us?

When you have checked in, you will be sent off for the security check, which is behind the check in desk. And then you take the escalator to the departure lounge. Most of the tour operator's desks are located at the end of the arrivals lounge but Ryan air is near the chemist in departures.

The departure lounge has plenty of places to buy reasonably priced food, which may be eaten on the sun terrace at either end of the departure lounge. There are also the usual duty free shops.

Fuerteventura Airport Shopping.

As you get through security at the airport, which is on the ground floor. The first shop that you will see is a store selling traditional items from Fuerteventura. As you go up the escalator you will find a wide range of shops selling duty free items and clothing. There are several cafes and you can take a relaxing drink or snack on to the patio area and enjoy the last bit of Fuerteventura sunshine that you will see for a while.

It is important, for those of you that are not on a direct flight home that you get any duty free items sealed so that you will not be charged taxes at the next airport.

www.ingramcontent.com/pod-product-compliance
Lightning Source LLC
Chambersburg PA
CBHW021109080526
44587CB00010B/447